Steering the Mothership

The Complexities of Mothering

Lisa Cherry

Published by Spring Publishing,
an imprint of Careertrain Publishing

www.springpublishing.co.uk

hello@springpublishing.co.uk

Printed and bound in Great Britain

ISBN 978-0-9927587-1-4

Disclaimer

This guide is for information purposes only and is not intended as a substitute for legal or other professional services.

Readers are urged to consult a variety of sources and educate themselves fully. The information expressed herein is the opinion of the author, and is not intended to reflect upon any particular person or company. The author and publisher shall have no responsibility or liability with respect to any loss or damage caused, or alleged to be caused, by the information or application of the information contained within this guide.

"Children begin by loving their parents; as they grow older they judge them; sometimes they forgive them."

— Oscar Wilde, *The Picture of Dorian Gray*

Contents

Acknowledgments

I would like to thank all the people who have had little pieces of me, of my heart and of my soul that I had lost, or had been broken or that I could not find. All those little pieces that were shattered have almost all been found and handed back to me so I could finish off the repair job that recovery started all those years ago.

I must therefore start with Eunice Lumsden who writes the foreword in this book, the Social Worker I remember, the Social Worker I had for the longest time, the Social Worker who was professional through and through.

Next I have to acknowledge Craig Dobson who played a huge part in my care experience in the strangest of ways really, who I have recently been reconnected with and who, against every possible odds has not only stayed alive but now thrives.

Caroline Wills who I knew in my heart was important to me when I was a child but I wasn't sure why truly deserves a mention. I only discovered in what way she had left a mark upon me when I read my files from Social Services.

Rob Matheson who found me via Facebook and unknowingly and without meaning to, took me back to Craig Dobson; Rob is a true care brother who can be found with his voice and his guitar playing his wonderful music around the pubs of Northamptonshire.

All of these people have brought back to me a piece of myself that was a feeling; more often than not a memory with little imagery.

And of course there is Caroline Noble who brought me through the process of reading my files and who is searching right now for what feels like the very last bit of the jigsaw that is me; my father.

I must thank every person who came forward to contribute in this book, some of whom tried so hard to write about this intensely private space and found they couldn't. I thank everyone who was able to 'go there' to that place, the place that holds these particular experiences and trusting me to know how to work with this using the greatest care and respect.

My illustrator Joy Aitman, my graphic designer Steve Shepherd, Alison Thompson my proof reader and of course my publisher, Julie Cooper from Spring Publishing providing the team that pulls it all together.

Finally, but absolutely at the core of all my projects, Mr Smith and my lovely teens provide me with everything I need to explore my experiences, my challenges and areas that I need to grow. They support me in so many ways, enabling me to have the reserve to support others so that they can do the same.

Foreword

I was delighted when Lisa contacted me as part of her journey of discovery, and I'm honoured to be asked to write this foreword to *Steering the Mothership.*

I have rich memories of being Lisa's social worker, and of the challenges of a young person who was very much in charge of *steering* herself through the complexities of being 'in care'. In reality, I was one of many professionals who played a small part in her life's journey, yet our decisions and actions shaped how Lisa felt about herself, how she experienced life, and the decisions she made. It is interesting the different lenses we each bring to our memories: she recalls the labels she was given, while I recall a bright and able young woman who was 'angry' - rightly - about her situation. Indeed, I was often angry on her behalf.

Lisa's advocacy skills were already evident as a young person; she challenged the system then and she does so today. She was a young person who was going to be a social worker and make things different. Those who have read her previous books or who know Lisa will agree that she is succeeding; she has a real gift for presenting her search for self in a way that speaks to others. She is able to locate the personal in a wider context of research and policy, to give her work acuity.

Furthermore, the question Lisa addresses in this book - why it has taken so long to make the connection between her birth and her innermost feelings - is highly pertinent. It addresses the importance of 'Mother', and the power of the inter-generational relationship between parent and child. It also reinforces the vital importance of a child's early years and positive attachments.

This is a strong and important message that needs to be heard: earliest experiences are critical, including the nature of how we are conceived. The impact of interrupted childhood on later life outcomes can be immense. Valuing those early years is vital - as is having knowledgeable, skilled professionals who understand the importance of attachment and relationships. I know when you read this book you will be impressed with how Lisa is able to present her experiences of this in a way that holds meaning for others.

Like all those I had the privilege of working with as a social worker, Lisa played a part in shaping my own professional life. We were 'professionals' that Lisa could not remember the names of - though I do take some pride in the fact that she remembered me and how I made her feel. Lisa has given me an opportunity to reflect and ponder how we do (or do not) support children and young people in the care system. More importantly, she has led me to consider why we do not learn from the messages we are given and then use them to help shape a different future.

Lisa's contact with me was timely in my own professional journey. At different ages and stages in our lives we seek different things - the timing has to be right. I was focusing on the key questions you must ask when you dig deep to manage services for children, young people and families: why do you do what you do? What is your primary driver? What has influenced you? What will you compromise on and what will you NOT compromise on? These questions are necessary for a professional to manage the complexities of working in services that can be more engaged with professional politics than with the lives they are meant to support.

This recent contact with Lisa was something I had expected for many years – and in many ways I wish it had come earlier– but there is an important message here about timing. As Rumi the Turkish philosopher states: *"What you search for is searching for you."*

I do hope that what you are searching for is searching for you in the pages of this book.

Dr. Eunice Lumsden
University Teaching Fellow, Head Of Early Years, University of Northampton

Introduction

This is the book I never thought I could write. This is the book that terrified me when I started to think about how I would get my words onto the page. Writing about motherhood filled me with terror because the one area of my life that I couldn't reconcile, no matter how hard I tried, was the relationship that I didn't have with my own mother.

But something happened to me on Mother's Day 2013, something that had never occurred before. Previously, I had managed to get through many a Mother's Day either by ignoring it, tolerating it or accepting it and trying to deal with it. I celebrated myself as a mother with my own children, but I was unable to be a daughter and to have been mothered. But on this day, it was different as I woke up weeping – not only because I saw myself as the mother, but because I had started to understand my own experience of having a mother in a completely different way.

I started to write, to pour my words onto the page in a bid to understand what was tearing through my body. I felt a powerful surge of shame and pain and distress as I wrote a blog called How To Become A Mother and then shared it on my website.

What happened next is what gave birth to this book because, in understanding something within me about this deeply complex relationship, I received endless texts, emails, messages and replies to my post. In an instant, they gave me the knowledge that writing about this was something that I absolutely had to explore, whether I was ready to do so or not.

The mail that was sent to me represented the depth of emotion for mothers lost, for mothers who never mothered, for mothers who were relying on partners to acknowledge their huge contribution – that of raising the next generation – to the world on a macro and micro level. There were so many messages of connection, pain, loss, hurt and joy that I knew in that moment that this had to be my next book.

If you've read any of my other books you might ask why I wouldn't have explored this intricate relationship first, before all other explorations. Like most children of parents who haven't been able to look after them for whatever reason, I felt a loyalty and I didn't want to cause hurt and upset to my own mother, were she ever brave enough to read my writing. When I wrote about adults who had lived through the care system, I can tell you that every single person in that book wanted to protect their mother first, and then the rest of their family. Either they made that explicit by telling me that they did not want to talk about that relationship, or they merely omitted to mention their mother in their interview. The most anyone would say was that they did not have a relationship with their mother and therefore there was little to say in that regard. Loyalty was fierce, even when someone had been used by their mother to be abused by men in return for love. Complexity doesn't even begin to explain the myriad of emotions that are alive in this setting.

This observation of loyalty gave birth to the second epiphany that came to me, allowing me to write this book: the relationship between baby/child and mother is a complex, visceral, intensely private and often unarticulated aspect of each person. We are all born from The Mother. It is the beginning. It is therefore everything before there is anything else.

I came to realise that I hadn't developed a deep enough understanding about this to help me make sense of it; in terms of revelations, far more was to come. By writing this book I seek to explore this. My intention is to help the reader to better understand their own relationship as a mother and as a child of The Mother.

So what changed, and why now? Nothing changed and everything changed all at once. Having learnt the gift of sharing stories that enable connection, it seemed absolutely necessary that this relationship be explored. Why now? Because I have been on the planet long enough to understand more than I ever have about people, relationships, the good, the bad and the beautiful.

For some, making sense of this relationship can take a lifetime. How do we do that? One way is by allowing ourselves the chance to explore the relationships that work, and those that don't.

I seek to tell stories: the untold stories[1], the difficult aspects of life where there is often no platform for making known what we feel so deeply inside.

This is not a book about blame or pages of ranting and anger and despair. Neither is it a book that is an academic reference or an exhaustive list of all that there is to say.

There are also many untold stories of mothering. I have chosen to share the stories of those who came to me when I announced I was starting the project. This way I trust that exactly the right people for the book will come forward. I could have approached it in a much more journalistic way and sought out people with specific stories that I might wish to include but I feel that working in the way that I do creates a certain authenticity about it and fits in with my view of the world.

All the contributors are women. I feel that I am getting closer to writing with men and sharing their stories but so

---

[1] Nearly all of the contributors have asked for their identity to be concealed through changing identifiable details and their names.

far I have not found men who are comfortable writing about their emotional space in this format. I am certain that this will change and that the opportunity will arise that allows me to do that but for whatever reason, it is not now and it is not here.

What I do offer you is a book about the complexities of mothering and how we start to understand ourselves as mothers and as children of The Mother, while exploring the essential need for The Mother to have the best possible opportunity she can with her baby/child from conception, thereby seeking to ensure that trauma can be limited for both.

My purpose is to understand what happens to us, how it affects us and ultimately how we heal from our experiences.

PART ONE

Steering the Mothership

Chapter One

Life is messy – a complex web of perception and understanding, underpinned by a unique set of people, circumstances and events that create the fabric that is life. And it is because of that that I have written this chapter several times while going through huge changes and shifts in my own understanding about mothering. Little did I know how much would change when I embarked upon this particular leg of the journey in terms of the learning I have gained, which has enabled me to understand myself at a level far deeper than I could have hoped for.

Creating this work has also allowed me to unfold my own personal journey of forgiveness, compassion and understanding with my mother where there had previously been only anger and distance. Whilst the learning that I have undertaken has given me that, it has also brought me to a place where I accept that there will always be distance, physically and emotionally. I can live in that place but now I can be there without the anger.

In this book, we can start to explore and understand Mother as the social construct that it is, dependent on the era, location, society, the class/sexuality/marital status of the woman, the politics of that time. It is mothering itself that I am interested in. The 'doing' of mothering. And beyond that, the 'doing' of mothering that is often not spoken of, so there are many reflections in here from the child's adult perspective. Messy, complicated, taboo, disconnected, uncomfortable, real, painful and often hidden.

So what is my starting point? Well, I have been an abandoned baby, grandchild in situ, a stepchild, a child in care, living in foster homes and residential units, nobody's child. I have been a single mother, a married mother, a stepmother, a mother in a relationship. I have also worked extensively for over two decades with adults and children who have led their entire lives shaped by their experiences of being – or not being – mothered, or of being a mother struggling to do so. There is no other relationship that is so life-forming, defining and shaping.

My assertion is that the relationship between The Mother and baby is completely unique and cannot be replicated. The Mother is the beginning, before there is anything else. It offers a period of time that excludes all others; from the moment of conception through to the cutting of the cord there is no one else present in this relationship. The hearts beat as one, in sync, silently while they both start to get to know each other.

There are a number of books that explore the universal complexities within the relationship between child and mother. There are also endless texts that offer a traditional look at mothers, babies, parenting and all that this throws up on a daily basis as we weave our way through this maze of a life-changing event. What should we feed them? When should they sit up/crawl/walk/talk, etc?

Steering The Mothership is an exploration of and an opportunity to understand the pain that is felt when there is loss, grief, guilt, shame, abandonment and isolation. It looks at how this relationship shapes our lives in the life circle and how we can go on to heal, grow and ultimately break the cycle of pain.

I have read many things about the relationships we have with our mothers and the types of mothers that there allegedly are, a lot of which focus on the mother as 'bad' or 'good'. This is generally an approach of duality that our society takes when it can't understand things or, I would also argue, when it can't 'control' things. The domain of the mother is a female space and as such has been subject to the same lack of input, connection and importance as anything else in a society that does not place value upon women. However, women have sons, of course, so again, as with much of what is deemed as unimportant, this affects us all.

I have seen many books that seek to label the 'types' of mothers 'available', including the narcissistic mother, the inadequate mother, the abusive mother and so on.

In the dualistic world of 'good' and 'bad', the 'bad' mother construct tells of a woman who doesn't want her child, can't connect with her child and can't take responsibility for her child. For a long time – and this still pervades our culture now – the 'bad' mother is usually a single mother. She can come from any ethnic background and is probably likely to be working class. Her sexuality will be gay or straight. She might have a disability.

The 'good' mother construct is most definitely heterosexual and married, probably doesn't work (or works part time), is white and middle class and helps out at the school with reading groups.

I don't wish to explore these constructs any further here but this simplistic view of a mother is never far away from us, even in a changing society, and will always have a part to play in how agencies respond to and work with mothers.

My mother was the 'bad' mother and essentially, although this was playing out from deep within my sub-conscious as well as my conscious thinking, I was the 'bad' child.

While the impact of this upon my life has diminished greatly after years of recovery and personal development work, it has never completely left me and it never gave me another lens through which I could view our experiences.

What I'm saying here is that all the therapy in the world as an adult could not touch the deep, visceral, inaccessible space created within me as an abandoned baby with a disturbed bond. Therapy was not enough. Not one person from whom I sought help, nor my own professional training, could give me the information I needed to heal.

However, there were two things I knew instinctively, without question and without exploration. Firstly, when I became a mother myself and I sat on the floor with my newborn son who I was soothing through my own tears of exhaustion, as I gazed deeply into his eyes and connected with him as only a mother and baby can, I knew that I had never been on the receiving end of that depth of connection with another human being. How could I know that? How could I possibly, in that moment, truly and with acceptance, know that?

Secondly, I knew that in order to heal my own feelings about not being mothered, I needed to become a mother myself and heal the damage within me through my love and connection with my own children. Often I have heard teenage girls from difficult backgrounds talk about having a baby so they had someone who would love them. My drive to be a mother was not to have someone who loved me but rather that I had someone who I could love. In doing so, I would be able to heal some of the trauma and pain that had yet to be explored and named; heal and recover.

Both of these things were instinctive; they were not rational thoughts, I had not read these things. I had no friends with babies at that point and had not been around 'mothering' at all on a personal level. And yet I knew these things to be true.

What I also knew to be true was that I was just a woman having a baby; not 'bad' nor 'good' nor any other label that attempts to define the space of mothering. I knew that I had little or no support. I didn't know what I needed and if I had, I wouldn't have known who to ask for it. I had created my baby with a man I had no interest in, lived in a flat rather than a community, and was without family.

Becoming a mother is far more complex than we are ever led to believe, although many times I have wished that I could have understood the roadmap of meeting someone, falling in love and creating a life of love and support together. But I was in my twenties and had gotten as far as I had with no roadmap to get me anywhere. I didn't understand how it all worked, what it all meant and how on earth I could make beautiful things such as loving relationships happen for me. For now, it was just me and my baby exploring our unique bond.

*

Chapter Two

My own entry into the world, and what followed thereafter, is what has created the person I am today; the person who has been on a personal journey that allowed this deep exploration that I want to share with you.

I arrived into this world in 1970 to an unmarried mother, pregnant at 20, living with her own mother who was a widowed French Catholic. My mother had gone and done the inconceivable and got herself pregnant, bringing utter shame to herself when anyone dared to ask what the bump was under the big red cape. A boyfriend, a few drinks, an evening out in Wigan and boom ... There's a baby coming. It could have happened to anyone, of course, but if you were a woman at that time, society was not in a position to accept this and judgement hung over the happy event like a dirty blanket.

'The bastard, like the prostitute, thief and beggar, belongs to that motley crowd of disreputable social types which society has generally resented, always endured. He is a living symbol of social irregularity.' Kingsley Davis, 'Illegitimacy and the Social Structure' (reprinted 1964), p.21.

Such beliefs about unmarried women having babies are hard to imagine in the context of today's society, for while there are remnants of these views still present, they are nothing compared to what they were back then. A woman getting pregnant out of marriage had made a terrible mistake. I must also add that she was deemed to have been 'bad' and was filled with shame about this terrible thing she had done (as if getting pregnant was solely her fault).

The expectation for a long time was that a baby born into this circumstance would be better off being adopted, and the amount of babies who were adopted peaked in the late 1960s, reflecting this view.

In this context, the solution was to be a Catholic one and at eight months pregnant my mother took the journey on what I imagine was a cold January day from Southport in the north west of England to Nazareth House in Wrexham, one of the last homes for unmarried mothers. Cold, judgemental, punishing and emotionless. I can only guess it was like this from research I have undertaken in writing this book. It may have been warm, welcoming, caring and open-minded, but I suspect not.

Homes for unmarried mothers were born under the guidance of The Salvation Army[2] which was founded by William Booth, an Evangelical Christian. The organisation became involved in a number of social welfare activities

---

[2] More information on The Salvation Army can be found on http://www.salvationarmy.org.uk/

alongside its religious crusading. Riding on the back of The Poor Relief Act of 1601, there were originally workhouses for prostitutes, the poor, the homeless and the sexually abused, but in 1891 in Hackney, Ivy House was opened by the daughter-in-law of William Booth himself. This was the very first mother and baby home.

This explains why religion has always been a thread running through mother and baby homes. By 1968, 58% of the homes were run by the Church of England, 11.6% by Roman Catholics, 5.3% by The Salvation Army, 3.5% by Methodists, and the remaining by other churches or local authorities.[3]

The history of the workhouses[4] and mother and baby homes is an interesting one that isn't for any further exploration here, but in it we are provided with an understanding of the underlying philosophy of the mother and baby home, and a comprehension of what type of policy and belief system it was created from. This enables us to better understand what type of environment women were entering during this era. Even though it would have been a far cry from the workhouses, it would still have been grounded in the idea that this was a place of shame,

---

[3] Nicholson, J. (1968). Mother and Baby Homes: A Survey of Homes for Unmarried Mothers. London: George Allen & Unwin Ltd.
[4] An interesting website called The Workhouse by Peter Higginbotham explores the history and work in some detail http://www.workhouses.org.uk Peter has written a number of books on the subject for further reading.

of poor, of lack and therefore of you not deserving to have your baby.

Societal beliefs in 1969/1970 around having a baby out of wedlock are best described as being 'shameful'. The words penance, shame and reformation are used a lot in the articles and interviews I have read on the subject. What is very interesting is that 'shame' is something that I talk about a lot in so much of my writing about recovery. Babies like me are conceived into it, born into it and then live it out through the aftermath of what happened to us once we were born. I have spoken many times of the red cape that my grandmother proudly made for my mother to 'hide the baby'. Hiding the baby was essential during this era and the fact that my grandmother could sew such a garment allowed a little reverse pride in dealing with this 'shameful' situation.

I will always remember the red cape and I wasn't even born during its existence.

*

Nazareth House, very early in 1970, was a large imposing house with little to say and much to be done; light housework awaited the women who were predominately teenagers or in their early twenties. Feeling ashamed, doing housework and giving birth were the order of the day. Adoption was seen as being ultimately the best option for all; best for the baby, best for society. It was expected.

This was the environment where my mother would finish her pregnancy, have her baby, hand over her baby for adoption and leave after just a few weeks, returning to work very quickly after giving birth.

The women arrived understanding that they would be giving up their babies for adoption and that to not do so would be selfish. As I mentioned earlier, 1968 – just before I was born – saw a peak in babies being adopted and 16,164 were.[5] It's highly possible that had I been born just months earlier, I would have been subject to what is often described of as 'forced adoption', but by 1970, mother and baby homes were closing fast.

*

In this setting, believing that your baby would be removed, taken away from you, that you were not worthy, that you had done something 'bad', it might be fair to suggest that attempting to dissociate from that baby would have to be tried. It is likely that the baby would have been denied, hidden, willed out of its own existence. Why would you partake in attaching to 'something' that was going to be taken away? Why would you dare to dream – as mothers dream – about what it would be like to look at your baby and gaze into their eyes after waiting nine months to meet them? Why would you do that? How painful would that be?

---

[5] Half A Million Women by Howe, Sawbridge and Hinings

I have read in various places and accounts from women who stayed in these homes that breastfeeding – which is well researched and documented as a way of attaching to your baby – was not allowed. Babies were also left for long periods in 'nurseries' without connection to other human beings. In terms of ensuring that a mother would not attach to her baby, thereby attempting to make the adoption 'easier', the workers in these homes knew what they were doing. What they didn't know – or didn't want to know – was the long term damage that this forced separation would have, not just on the mother when the child was removed from them but also on the baby.

I was that baby. I was that abandoned baby in the nursery – even though I was not to be adopted in the end. I understand this to be my first trauma. I don't know what the reality of the trauma was for my mother at this time, being parted from her baby, as we have never had that conversation, but the trauma that was suffered by my mother had a resolve of sorts as I was returned to her.

*

I researched Nazareth House, curious as to whether there was a way I could find any paperwork kept on my mother and me. Any old scrap of information that might provide one of the many missing parts of my life would do. Yet all I could find was an unobtainable phone number, and that Nazareth House was now a home for the elderly. What I also found, scattered across the internet, was the unspoken emotion of 1970 in the form of endless messages from children and mothers looking to be reunited after adoption.

I had typed 1970 into Google: my search engine, my friend, full of missing jigsaw pieces. I am certain if I had put any other year in, I would have found the same messages of despair, pieced together with shards of hope. Snippets of information scattered desperately across page after page in the faint hope that the missing piece of their heart might be searching too. I felt an instant sadness and connection all at once.

The assumption being I would be adopted, as my mother was unclear whether she would be able to keep me, I was removed from my mother soon after birth and placed into foster care, where all my practical needs were met – and not much more.

Back then it wasn't the way of things in terms of understanding babies, and it may well have been seen as inappropriate to connect emotionally with a baby that would be placed for adoption in a different family. Alongside arriving into shame and judgement, I had also arrived into an emotionless, disconnected human experience; I now understand that I was an abandoned baby and that this would shape me as a person in the most profound of ways.

Throughout this book I will seek to explore the impact of this during my life and the lives of the contributors, but what followed for me was an adolescence fraught with rage and deep feelings of 'not belonging'. When I was 13 I struggled to cope with those feelings of loss from having no attachment to another human being for the first six weeks of my life. I was also told that my natural father was dead. I was exhibiting fairly standard teenage behaviour and making full use of being left alone for a huge amount of the time, yet two bin liners were filled up with my things and given to Social Services by my mother as she demanded I be taken into care.[6] Self-medication took hold of me in the form of alcohol, which (fortunately) led me to an early recovery journey and sobriety from the age of 20.

However, as I mentioned earlier, even with recovery and therapeutic intervention there was still something missing. The anger I carried towards my mother was with me at all times and my relationship choices strayed into the bizarre, to say the least. I chose to have my children with someone I didn't have a relationship with. Why would I risk being with someone I loved who would abandon me when I would need them to support me as a mother? I see this as a process of 'non-attachment' to the extreme; very unhealthy, yet very emotionally safe and a place where I could remain detached and focused on mothering which, of course, I saw as vital.

---

[6] The Brightness of Stars: Stories of Adults Who Came Through The British Care System was published in 2013

I then went on to marry someone who had an eight month affair with a woman at work in the early stages of our relationship and who had a family who didn't want him to be with me and made that explicitly clear. Of course I would forgive him and of course they might accept me eventually. Rejection and abandonment issues are easier to see here. Essentially, without knowing it, he offered me what I *believed* was the security and stability I craved (a security and stability that I didn't even realise I wanted, rather strangely) and once I'd smelt it and touched it, I didn't want to let it go. I would see this as a process of 'toxic attachment'; also unhealthy, but safe yet again in that it wasn't complete; it was always going to end, it was fuelled by rejection, so the abandonment cycle could be fulfilled in that sense and was actually 'comfortable' to me, albeit unconsciously.

It was the end of that marriage, instigated by him leaving over Sunday dinner that triggered in me what I knew had been there all along, but was so far from my reach that I had done everything I could possibly do to ignore it. The igniting of the explosion waiting to happen, a space of loss and abandonment, a huge pool of unspoken and unarticulated words and emotions was now exposed. This took me to my knees and to a place of deep aloneness and started the journey that I now know, in one form or another, I had been avoiding all my life: the journey back to me. The journey back to the very beginning.

As the abandonment and loss detonated within me, my anger towards my mother intensified. While I had never gone to her for support in my life, when I did talk to her about what had happened I was bombarded with blame for the end of my marriage with no support whatsoever and it added to the feelings I was already dealing with. Even though they were feelings that I had yet to articulate, I knew somewhere within that they were all linked to this core relationship: the one I had, or didn't have, with my mother.

I decided to create a silence between us for at least two years, which was most welcome for us both, I think. It gave me some space to remove myself from the anger-guilt-shame cycle that I was in with regards to 'us'.

During those two years the anger diminished greatly but I was still grappling with feelings of being let down and feeling abandoned, and I couldn't seem to move away from it. There was clearly so much work to do and I wasn't sure which way to turn.

At some point during the course of the next couple of years I regained contact with my mother, developed my sense of compassion towards her, requested and received my files from Social Services and started the search for my father. This part of my recovery became something far more intense than I had felt before and completely changed the way that I understood the world, not only through my personal lens but also professionally.

Chapter Three

How did I develop my sense of compassion from a place of such loss and abandonment? One day, without warning or incident, I woke up and the way I felt about my mother had changed. I wish I could say an event happened or we had some sort of powerful conversation that meant we met up and we understood each other in that moment, but I literally just woke up and felt completely differently. This powerful internal shift had absolutely nothing to do with her; it was all within me. Compassion and forgiveness are never about the other person. This really crystallised what can be a trite and often difficult concept to understand when dealing with deep hurt into something that I could feel and see for myself.

This is also a powerful example of how not all intense shifts within us, in our thinking and in our feeling, come with a bang or a boom or a trauma or a crisis. Much of what I have learnt has usually appeared in the most massive of transitory times: the end of a relationship, early recovery, an illness, childbirth, loss. But this came in the silence, the quiet and the stillness. It supports a very recent part of my journey that has learnt to incorporate stillness into my life. It may be that I will go on to find that it is within the stillness that the most powerful shifts do take place.

I believe these shifts within the stillness are taking place in the subconscious part of ourselves, which is why they are calmer, more powerful and require stillness to access. If, as I said earlier, my trauma was located in my subconscious, an imprint on my soul, then conscious means of accessing it were no longer what I needed to get there. I shall explore this more deeply when we move on to how we can heal from our trauma.

Exploring the relationship with my mother in the context of being in a supportive, loving and safe relationship certainly played its part and made a huge difference to what I was prepared to feel and not feel. I was now living with the man I was to marry: a man who accepted me exactly as I was, who I trusted implicitly and who had been on a journey with me in terms of helping me to heal from all that had gone on before. Finally I felt like recovery from The Mother was a possibility for me.

Delving as deeply as I needed to do, and as I seemed to be directed to do from each encounter that I had, meant that I needed to have a lot of support around me and provide myself with good self-care. Again, I will explore self-care later on when we talk about healing from trauma.

The years and years of personal therapeutic work, both formal and informal, also travelled with me to this point and, I can only assume, placed me in a position that meant I was ready to deal with whatever was to come next in this part of my personal journey.

Within this quiet state of compassion and forgiveness that I felt towards my mother, I immediately wrote her a card saying that I wanted her to know I felt at peace with our relationship and that I wasn't angry any more.

Of course this was received with such delight, with which I was pleased. I suspect that this was interpreted as a possibility that we could now happily be mother and daughter, as if all of what had gone before hadn't happened and everything was going to be 'normal'. Being 'normal' is an important thing to my mother but it's not something I have ever really given a shit about so I was always going to disappoint in that regard.

Peace had been given to me. I felt peace. The anger appeared to have left me. My need for my mother to be a mother to me had passed.

I believe that there were fundamental reasons why this happened right now at this point in my life.

1. I was comfortably into my 40s, a time where a deeper understanding about life and our core relationships becomes easier to understand as we have travelled the life path for a while. This seems to be a part of what I now believe to be a stage of development in its own right. It's no accident that the people who came forward to take part in this book were predominately past the age of forty.

2. My own children were at that time 14 and 16 years old and the mirror was reflecting back to me of my own adolescence, my own failings, my own successes. My beautiful, talented, challenging, demonstrative teenagers were emerging into the adults they would become in front of my very eyes while locked into all of the things that they needed to deal with during their adolescence.

3. I understood for the first time that this was not about forgiveness after all, but about compassion.

4. I started to verbalise and research the trauma that had been suffered when we were separated for six weeks from the moment I was born while she explored whether keeping me was going to be a possibility for her as a single mother and a Catholic daughter in 1970.

The first two points are fairly self-explanatory. 'Midlife', as being post 40 years old has often been described, is almost a stage of development all of its own as we shift and change, forget and forgive and often soften. I feel it is a movement from one part of our lives into another, often a transitory phase which leads people to change jobs, careers, partners and countries of residence. It's often seen as dramatic or a crisis by onlookers, but by the individual concerned it can feel like a necessity to lead a life that makes more sense, has more fulfilment and purpose.

It's an opportunity to reflect, to grow, to 'find' ourselves and to start to understand our immortality in a different way.

With regards to my own teenagers going through their own personal journeys, wading through the emotional quagmire that is adolescence, rebelling and searching and growing and risk taking, my own parental needs became focused on what they took into adulthood. Yes, on a practical level they needed passports and driving licences and an education (all the things I had had to provide myself with as Nobody's Child), but I was also helping them navigate their own experiences and trying to help them understand themselves.

I believe that it is through parenting our teenagers consciously that we can really begin to understand ourselves and the world around us. It's possible that that is why 'youth' is so feared, and has been historically since records of 'youth' have been kept; why they are so ignored, deemed to be so challenging. There is no greater mirror than your teenage child.

The latter two points about forgiveness and trauma take rather more explaining. In my first book Soul Journey[7], I

---

[7] Soul Journey: The Greatest Secrets to Living The Life You Want was published in 2012

explore forgiveness as being key to recovery[8] and I still believe that forgiveness is a concept that needs to be integrated into any kind of journey to find peace from pain. However, forgiveness for me now feels like the top layer in this process. Yes, terrible things had happened to me because of my mother's inability to parent me, very terrible things that had plagued me all my life. But she had also had to deal with difficult things. She was just a person who got pregnant. Now while I had always known this in a cognitive way, the cycle of feelings that followed meant I couldn't get to a place where I could understand myself effectively enough to do something about it, or get to a place where I could speak about it with my mother and essentially start to repair some of the damage.

So the cycle that kept me in a place of anger towards my mother, even when I was going through a daily process of forgiveness for well into two decades, looked something like this diagram.

---

[8] By recovery, I mean whatever it is we are recovering from rather than just as a word used to describe recovery from alcoholism and/or addiction.

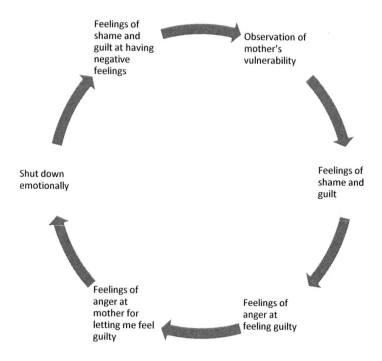

This cycle meant that whenever I wanted to contact her, this process occurred within me on an almost subconscious level and I didn't know how to make it stop. I felt that she was happy for me to support her in not taking responsibility for me as a child and for what had subsequently happened thereafter. When I saw her as 'vulnerable' I couldn't move on because I kept getting stuck in guilt; guilt because I was so cross with someone who clearly hadn't the tools to do things differently. Understanding this cycle really helped me to see where my blocks were.

Chapter Four

The letter I sent my mother explaining the peace that I had now found had a domino effect on me clearing out the last bits of debris within myself – all the things I had never wanted to look at.

I set about arranging a meeting with a social worker that I remembered I had had for most of my time in care as a young teenager.

I also applied to the County Council that had been my Corporate Parent during my time in their 'care' and requested that I be able to read my files. I wanted to read my files not because I cared about the perceptions of others of me at a very difficult and challenging of my life, but because I wanted to understand more about how I ended up in care in the first place.

The first thing that came to fruition on this new path of my Journey To Self was that I met with Eunice. I remember her as a 'feeling' rather than a person and I think that is how it should be in the context of Social Worker or Teacher. An important person in your life at a time when your life consumes you means that they have to be remembered as a feeling. A quote I often recall as a favourite is Maya Angelou's:

"I've learned that people will forget what you said, people will forget what you did, but people will never forget how you made them feel"

That felt very relevant when thinking about Eunice.

My meeting with Eunice was quite remarkable in that her memory of me and the details of my 'case' were stunning. Back in the mid-1980s she was a young, enthusiastic, newly qualified social worker, yet to have her own children, whose notes I believed would be very comprehensive and thorough so I felt that meeting her would be helpful on many levels prior to reading my files!

We exchanged a few emails, during which time she stalked me for a while (her words) and performed some checks on what I was doing and whether meeting me would pose a risk to her. Once she was satisfied that meeting me would be a good idea, we finally agreed to meet for a coffee.

We arranged to meet in a pretty country pub. It was August and it was a beautiful summer's day so we could sit outside. I recognised her instantly, much to my surprise, as I wouldn't have known it were her had we walked past one another in the street prior to meeting that day.

She had brought me a gift, which I opened later when home alone: Russian dolls nestled in a mosaic candle holder. As we settled into our conversation her knowledge and remembrance of the detail of 'me' was quite astounding.

I asked her the questions I needed answers to almost instantly. Why didn't Social Services try and work with me and my mother to return me home? And if they had, would it have been possible? It was clear in her mind that I would not have been able to go home. My mother was unable to parent me, to put my needs first, to set boundaries and the damage done prior to me going into care was extensive.

Eunice believed strongly that the place I needed to begin was at the very beginning: the place where there had been a severed attachment between my mother and me. She suggested some books I could read that might help me understand what had happened at that time. This was interesting to me as the very beginning had not been a place that I had explored in any great depth. How could I? I didn't remember it. I could feel it but I couldn't remember it. This seems strange to me now. The beginning is the beginning.

My application to the County Council who 'looked after' me went through pretty quickly. After an initially strange email interaction with someone from Data Protection who clearly had no idea how potentially traumatic this process might be, I was eventually put into contact with the team that dealt with such enquiries: The Post-Adoption Team. I wasn't entirely sure how I'd come to be in the hands of this team – and then I remembered. My mother had had a short and volatile marriage when I was ten years old and we had undergone the process of her husband adopting me.

The person who starting writing to me to arrange to bring me my files was a wonderful woman called Caroline. I was dreading two young social workers turning up who I would be cross with because they wouldn't have the knowledge, skill or wisdom that I felt I needed in order to be 'held' in this process. Two women, one of them Caroline, with more years and more experience than I, arrived at the door and I felt an internal sigh of relief.

A good friend had had the foresight to realise I may need to not be alone and had joined me for the meeting. After the pleasantries of coffee and chit chat, we sat down with my files and started talking through some of the things I might find and how I might feel about them. During this process it emerged that their team, being Post–Adoption, offers a service whereby they can search for parents. They said they would try and help me to find my dad. Emotion exploded out of me like projectile vomiting but with slightly less drama. Wow. Someone could help me. Someone with the resources to do this could look for the man who had been told I had been aborted and whose name may as well have been Tom Jones or Mark Smith.

With that news whirling around my body, I was passed my blue files. Having thought I would read them slowly and over time, I read them through in an afternoon underneath a blanket, with coffee and chocolate in hand. That was how I discovered what had happened. That was how I came to be poring over hand-written letters from my mother demanding I be fostered. That was how I learned how she actively tried to sabotage the foster placements while only wanting me to return to live with her in those periods where I was refusing to go back there; yet as soon as I tried to go 'home' she would change her mind. I read about the two bin bags of my belongings given to Social Services and the list of bad things I was supposed to have done that were far less than anything my own teenage children have done. I saw a child who was not parented and often not seen for days on end as my mother left the house before I was up and in the evenings we managed to avoid one another. It made me wonder who was feeding me.

My mother's hand-written letters, the social workers, the bin bags, my anger, my demise but not yet my rise – all that and more was in there. My issues of abandonment were not just to be explored in the context of my severed bond as a baby but also as a thirteen year old. My mother had abandoned me twice.

Before receiving my files I went to visit my mother to ask her how I ended up in care and to talk through some of things that had happened to me and maybe explore why she had made some of the decisions. She told me that she wasn't sure. She alluded to the possibility of another family member having something to do with it but other than that she didn't know. Even with me there, adult to adult, woman to woman, in the knowledge that I was going to be getting my files, she was unable to take responsibility for her actions. Even with me sitting in front of her with peace in my heart, she was still incapable of being the mother of the child.

Reading in my files what really did happen was probably the hardest thing for me to deal with. Yet again, she had let me down. Fortunately I recovered from this quickly but it made me think a lot about what reading files can bring up.

If you are reading this and you have the unique experience of being in a system that means someone has documented your very existence as a child and you would like to read about this, I would suggest to you that there are some things worth exploring within yourself first.

1. Make sure you are surrounded by loving, safe and non-judgemental support.
2. Think about what you want to know.
3. Think about how you might feel if you don't get the answers you desire.
4. Think about how you might feel if there are no answers.
5. Explore the possibility of you finding out things you don't want to know.

I have no regrets about reading my files at all and I'm glad that I did it at this point in my life and not before.

This process changed my understanding and shifted my perception about everything that had happened to me. I had the deepest compassion for myself in a way that I hadn't had before. My strength, resilience and determination as a person had masked a vulnerability for years and while I was now living comfortably with my vulnerability, this was different. Now I could see the 13 year old girl. Alone, confused, angry and hurt.

The world view I had of that 13 year old had been created by many other people and I had carried it through life as if it were mine. It was a view that told me that I was the 'bad' child, the angry teenager, the 'little shit' as it was once put so eloquently to me. The self-blame was rooted so deeply that it hadn't been touched by any of my professional or personal work. It was rooted so deeply that it explained much to me about the 'story' about myself I had carried around with me – even when I thought my 'stories' were completely different. I thought I had explored all of this. I thought I knew me better than this. This is incredibly powerful information to have in terms of the human condition and how we might process and store experiences.

This inner hidden 'story' was in one of those bin bags and the time had arrived to throw it out; I just needed to find it before I could dispose of it.

So the place to start was the beginning: the Source of Life. I had to explore different things than I had always thought I needed to know in my quest for understanding myself, healing my internal pain and thereby being able to help others.

Chapter Five

With my new-found knowledge in hand plus my desire to head to the 'Source of Life' to see what more I could learn and understand, I returned from my meeting with Eunice and started some research. Incidentally, I had already started writing *Steering The Mothership* and this journey of exploration changed the whole direction and much of the content of what I had started to write. That is how powerful my new discoveries were.

I ordered a number of books, all focusing on adoption and attachment. I had never thought to read about adoption and attachment in relation to my own experiences and how I might have been affected because my focus had always been on my teenage years and having been in care. What I now understand about that focus was that it had all been about self-blame, carrying and internalising the 'story' I had been fed by many people that I was a particularly difficult teenager.

I will return to the notion of the 'story' in the last section of the book but in short, I had believed that I had gone into care because I was out of control when in fact, while I was indeed an angry teenager, my behaviour was well within the confines of normal teenage behaviour. The deterioration came from going through the experiences that followed rather than being what took me into care in the first place. However, the anger that I felt came from somewhere and my explorations took me to a place of starting to understand myself on a much deeper level.

The first book that arrived was by Nancy Verrier and I sat and read the first few chapters in disbelief. So much of what she was describing was me. Fundamentally, she was describing the pain and hurt and the lifelong sense of loss and abandonment that was so much a part of me that it was integral to my very being.

Verrier states that it is her belief "...that the severing of that connection between the adopted child and her birth mother causes a primal and narcissistic wound, which affects the adoptee's sense of self and often manifests in a sense of loss, basic mistrust, anxiety, and depression, emotional and/or behavioural problems and difficulties in relationships with significant others. I further believe that the awareness, whether conscious or unconscious, that the original separation was the result of a 'choice' made by the mother affects the adoptee's self-esteem and self-worth." Verrier, The Primal Wound, 1993, P16[9]

All the reading I have undertaken on this subject asserts that the trauma felt in this separation is severe for the

---

[9] Nancy Verrier, author of The Primal Wound, which is how she describes the trauma felt by the adopted child.

mother and for the baby. I had suffered this trauma and as I have said, I don't know what trauma my mother suffered, as I returned to her at six weeks old and she has never spoken about it in any emotional depth. Even though I had returned to her, there is a very real possibility that she was unable to bond with me too. Both of us may have been left with that inability, not just me. However, that suffering had left a permanent mark on my soul that prior to now had not had a name, nor a means of understanding it.

There are many books about being adopted and indeed it has become a huge social concern for many as the story has unfolded about forced adoption and the effects on children and mothers in this process. However, what about those of us who arrived into that setting, were abandoned awaiting adoption but later returned to our mothers and still had the severed, disturbed bond thrust upon us? What happened to us? Who told us about how we could have been affected?

This led me to think further about the complications of mothering and how the same effects felt by the child that was removed from birth would surely be felt by any child who had been through this state of non-attachment. And then the penny dropped. This isn't about adoption; this is about the interrupted bond between a mother and her baby.

I started to wonder about women with severe post natal depression or mental health issues that prevented empathy, for example. It started to make sense to me that if we could understand the issues faced by children who had been adopted, we could extend this further. Even though I myself was not adopted, I identified so heavily in terms of what had happened to me, how I felt and the destroyed relationship between my mother and me, and yet no one had ever thought to explore this with me ... ever.

If that's the case, then we now have a powerful piece of knowledge indeed, and it was this penny dropping in my head that led me to assert that every person who came to me and asked to be a contributor would have, somewhere in their story, an interrupted bond; whether through adoption, post natal depression, being premature, where there were mental health issues. Somewhere, I believed, this resides in the history of a person who feels lost, abandoned, disconnected.

We can use this to understand that the nurture and care of the mother, the support networks required, the whole system around childbirth has to take account of this absolute need for the mother to be able to bond with her baby. Everything thereafter becomes a plaster to mask and then attempt to heal this initial harm, hurt or, as Verrier puts it, wound and trauma. There are some really good books around about this and much research to support the early years agenda based on this knowledge. [10]

*

My own pathway into motherhood was an interesting one. As I mentioned earlier I just knew that I wanted a baby. I didn't necessarily know that I wanted to be in a loving relationship with stability and create the cornflake packet family that I had never had. I just knew that I wanted a baby. In fact, I wanted a child. I wanted to be a mother. I didn't want something to love me, as I have often heard expressed; I wanted something to love so I could demonstrate what I wanted mothering to look like. I wanted to be the mother that I didn't have for myself. This sounds a little naïve as I look back. But that is how I felt when I got pregnant at 25 to a man I had no real affection for in any sense.

When I entered into motherhood, I had not yet explored much of what I know today about who I am and what healing I needed. I hadn't the first clue about what I was doing and I was mostly driven by instinct.

When my first baby arrived, I knew how to breastfeed, how to attach, how to stay focused on his needs, how to express my warmth and love and how to fiercely protect him from all others. I don't know how I knew all of that but

---

[10] Why Love Matters by Sue Gerhardt explore the relationship between development and cortisol, for example

I did – and thank goodness! I was completely isolated. I had no friends with babies, no siblings of my own. I had barely been near a baby if I'm honest, and I obviously had no mother to turn to – nothing. The man I had chosen to be the father of this baby had a family but I couldn't work out how to interact with them, let alone ask them for help or support. I am amazed by how I instinctively seemed to know many of the elements of mothering that I now know I hadn't experienced myself.

I bumbled my way through the early weeks and months, holding down a full time job as a Leaving Care Social Worker, slightly depressed and very exhausted, but always connected to my baby. Having had him for me, I now wanted another baby for him. I wanted him to have a sibling; I didn't want him to be alone as I was. And so again, I engineered the creation of baby number two with the man I didn't like very much and was pregnant again.

It was a very difficult pregnancy emotionally and I felt more and more isolated as I tried to juggle a toddler, an odd 'relationship' I didn't want, a full time job and a course. But then the most beautiful little girl popped out and again, my instincts kicked in and we gazed at each other for two whole hours straight after the birth. It's the most beautiful experience and one I won't forget. I have never felt as complete in my mothering as I did with a baby and a toddler in tow; mothering in its most exhausting, all-consuming blanket of pure unconditional love.

They are now well into their teenage years and through time they have taught me how to love, how to demonstrate that love, how to be the mother I wanted to have for myself. They show me who I am – whether I like what they are showing me or not. They are a mirror of all that I am. They have pushed me to my emotional limits and continue to do so every day. I adore them.

Not being mothered beyond receiving the gift of life, not being attached and being disposed of onto the streets with my two bin bags at the age of thirteen fuelled me to be the mother I am rather than hindered me. If I had to assign any possible evidence of having been to Mothering School to my family, it would have to go to my grandmother who, in the first few years of my life, did show me love and mothering and care. And for that I am very grateful.

*

The relationship between mother and child is fraught with expectation of how a mother should be and, often, how a child should be. And yet the process of becoming a mother, how it is construed and thereby constructed socially and the actual reality of mothering and of being mothered are all very different things, yet intertwined in a web of complexity.

Exploring this complexity needs to be brought to life or it remains out of sight and we only have the images portrayed to us in the media versus the confusion we feel inside. I used to loathe the covers of baby magazines that featured gorgeous, blooming pregnant women while I felt huge and sick and desperate. Bridging that gap can be tricky and that is before a baby is even born, along with all of the chaos that brings, both emotionally and physically.

Mothering is a highly emotive subject that pushes our buttons in the most unexpected of ways as we all try and make sense of our experience as the child and, for many of us, as the mother too. The cycle of life is observed through the understanding that it can be messy. More often than not the depth of these feelings is left unexplored.

There are a number of reasons for this: loyalty, protection, it being too painful, difficulty articulating it as often there are no words that describe the feelings with any real meaning.

One way to bring the variety of complexities to life is to share stories of others, written in their own words and drawing upon their own experiences and understandings. I have been astounded by the stories I received, and there were also people who felt that it was too much to bear. Too visceral, too deep, too much.

*

My hope for you as the reader is that you learn much about yourself and others during the process of reading the stories. It is also my desire that those of us who work with mothers and with children learn more about how what happens to us can shape and form the adult that lies ahead, whilst undertaking the path of recovery for ourselves.

PART TWO

The Complexities of Mothering

Chapter Six - Wendy

On being a mother, or how to break your own heart

"Some people need to be loved from a distance, for a time anyway. It doesn't matter, love doesn't know the difference anyway."

(Found on the internet)

It didn't start well. As with almost all other aspects of my life at the time, my pregnancy was unplanned.

Despite having been married for five years I was still surprised and embarrassed by the evidence of my fertility and sexual activity. My own mother said at the time I'd had a good run for my money by working class standards in the 1970s; I'd done some travelling, carried on with what was essentially a single person's life but with a husband I'd managed to persuade to come on an adventure or two with me. I was anchored to a way of life my sort of family had had for at least two generations that I knew of: limited, constrained and fettered by the need to work hard, bloody hard to make a living.

Whilst I was pregnant I struggled with my corporeality, yet another anchor to this world of flesh and ache. And as with

Marley's chests and chains I was pulled back to the earth, back to my swelling body, back to this reality with the burgeoning realisation that this thing inside me, this parasite that grew each day, was going to leave me by my most private parts. I was horrified, and angry, and stoic and very slightly fascinated.

I read books, looked at graphic images of women in stirrups presided over by doctors in white coats and nurses with the vicious look of the big girls in the playground. I went to maternity classes, lay on a mat holding my breath whilst a midwife with a stopwatch timed us; she said we'd need this skill in labour. I wanted to pass the test this time as they were the first classes I'd done since failing six of my eight O Levels seven years before. It seemed I had another chance to be good at something.

The night came, announced by a pinging, popping wash of liquid that soaked my bed and missed the bucket we peed in each night, our bedsit being three floors above the nearest toilet. We walked under stars in silence to an ordinary building that saw this ordinary extraordinary act repeated continually on a loop, the soundtrack the cries of women and babies, the occasional wail of the siren and the slow pacing of men in the corridor.

My firstborn arrived at three in the afternoon, emerging through her torn and bloodied mother's pain with a clear intelligence present as she fixed me with a blue-eyed stare. My measure was got; it didn't amount to much.

This wasn't an especially auspicious start but from my conversations with other new mothers I knew that it could have been very much worse, and indeed it was for many of them. But I also knew that whilst I found the process of being a mother and getting to know my daughter interesting, the enormity of this change wasn't something I had yearned and wished for as others around me did. Somehow I felt I was experiencing it all through cotton wool. During the birth I felt my psyche leaping out of my wrenching body, heading somewhere, anywhere rather than in that room, to do anything rather than wait for that event, and I didn't feel as though I had entirely reintegrated it. Looking back this saddens me. I wish that I could have looked forward to this, dared to admit my desire for it, embraced it, felt the fear rather than run from it, cried the tears rather than reabsorbed their bitter, salty drops.

From the start I seemed out of sync. All around me nurses, midwives, heath visitors, NCT teachers told me how well I was doing but I couldn't feed her, I couldn't let her lie with her mouth to my breast and attach those hungry lips to my nipple. When she managed through her tenacity and determination to latch on there was no let down. If my body was creating any milk it sure didn't want to let it go. Inside I could feel myself getting smaller with each attempt and the seductive safety of a rubber teat and glass bottle gave me the distance necessary for me to feed her. I remember the relief of finding that I could prop her up in a bean bag so that she didn't need me to hold her. I was a poor little girl with a poor little girl.

But I loved her too. It was a passionate affair, more passionate than any other love I had known. I was delighted by her beauty and cleverness. She was born with a full head of hair and when I took her out in her pram she attracted crowds to her side. She smiled, cooed and was cooed over. I was proud; I was enjoying her. I was also deeply scared of getting it wrong.

I devoured Baby and Child by Penelope Leach. I discovered my own particular parenting style of benign neglect – any food dropped on the floor was fair game for a hungry mouth so long as it wasn't wet; pyjamas were any clothes that were comfortable enough to sleep in; dummies were entirely acceptable (I was a working class girl, after all); getting all the saucepans out of the cupboard was a great game; a baby bath emptied of water, filled with toys could occupy a girl for at least twenty minutes.

From a very young age I read to her; this was my replacement for breastfeeding. Our strongest connection was made through the storybooks we read together, our mutual love of words and pictures reinforcing the bond between us. I remember this time with a smile and a sense of having snatched something very precious from a devouring fire. When I look at pictures from this time I see a beautiful child with a beautiful child; it not entirely clear who is in charge of who.

Two years into this journey I gathered enough confidence to embark on another pregnancy and with the benefit of the lessons learnt from the first time around gave birth to another daughter, this time easily and with no pain relief. It was a joyful event, looked forward to and celebrated; the contrast was striking. From the start I noticed this baby was easier to bond with. She seemed to like me, gloried in my presence. Making her smile was easy and she rarely stopped. I loved having two little girls; I felt like I was finally a good mum. We made an attractive package walking down the centre of the High Street, one girl on either side of me. This finally seemed to be an exam I had got an A in. My first.

But the relationship with my husband was fractured. Growing up is tough on young marriages and ours didn't survive. Somehow the blame for this, although in reality shared, was firmly heaped on my shoulders from my husband's perspective and my eldest daughter began to view me through this lens. I was pushed firmly from my pedestal and this did no one, least of all her, any favours. Our interactions, which had been put on a much firmer foundation, began to return to their earlier shakier counterparts. She was angry with me for the pain she felt about her parents splitting up and this anger, and the corresponding guilt and lack of confidence that were generated in me, began to build the walls that exist today in both of us.

Another relationship, and two more babies were added to the smiley girl and an eight year old who felt, to all intents and purposes, like a teenager crossed with a toddler: moods, temper tantrums, slamming doors, attempts to run away and silences, hard mutinous silences. I tried various techniques to manage this behaviour. Penelope Leach hadn't written anything about teenagers but if she had I would have devoured it. I searched for a key to unlock the sweet vulnerable thing I knew was inside her. I told myself that no matter what, I would be there for her. I told myself that it wasn't her fault that it was probably mine – and the look on her face confirmed this. No family event or expedition was complete without a scene that placed her at the centre of the action. I remember at times trying to express just what was upsetting and angering me so much about her attitude – "It's your tone of voice, the way you say things, just as if I was something dirty on the bottom of your shoe." She would turn and stare, her mute response triggering a spill of words from my mouth, generating the indelible impression in me of myself as Rumpelstiltskin, stamping and spitting at the end of her bed until I fell through the floorboards to hell below. She would turn on her side and go back to sleep.

Throughout this period, which went on for so many years I lost count, and just like at the beginning of her life, I felt out of sync. People told me what a good mother I was, how they admired my approach with my children and what lovely people I was growing. Somehow that didn't cut it when I knew something was not right with my eldest. She was the first thing I thought about in the morning and the last thing at night. My other three children became shadow puppets in the daily dramas; they had a part to play but they were rarely the stars of their own shows. I was stretched beyond elasticity, scraped thin as margarine on dry white bread. There was no respite, no soft eyes. I could not reach her, ever. Eventually I stopped trying. I told myself that's what she wanted. I knew it wasn't true but I felt helpless and impotent.

And yet, strange as it might seem, the connection between us was of the deepest kind. It was the kind where you are no longer sure where you start and the other finishes. Leaving home was hard for her. She hung on and on, went to university and had to come back again two short weeks later. She went and came back the most out of all of my children – the last two times, home to roost and to lick the wounds of a relationship that promised the world and delivered two children. The tragic irony is that it is because of this closeness that communication is impossible. I know where she's coming from, she knows what will come out of my mouth before I say it and we drive each other crazy with this knowledge. She enters a room full of a dark power, able to empty it of friendly faces with a look and a carefully chosen barb. I am powerless to help her get what she wants.

The fact of my difficult relationship with my daughter gnawed away at me, eating through my confidence, my knowledge of myself as a good person. Yet again I saw myself as I thought she saw me with those bright blue eyes, and it wasn't flattering. I felt those eyes reflected someone who had failed in one of the primary relationships in her life. This sense spread like a cancer through me, infecting how I viewed all of my children's childhoods. I could no longer look at photographs of them and their playtimes; it was too painful to look through those eyes. I did not trust myself any longer. My responses were always studied and calculated; I had to guard what I really felt, bury it so deep I didn't even really know what it was I felt. I had no access to my creativity and my world became smaller and smaller. I was dying, slowly dying, and I felt bad.

Eventually things became so uncomfortable in my head I knew I had to get help. I enrolled on a confidence-building course. I don't know why I thought I needed it but I knew I needed to change something and this seemed as good a place to start as anywhere. The process I went through encouraged me to look at key events in my life through new eyes, ones that weren't quite so damning of myself. I looked a little more kindly and more forgiving at the past. It encouraged some distance when regarding my daughter's behaviour, and reminded me that although she might be behaving like a hurt eight year old she was actually now a thirty-two year old mother of two. It helped me off my hook, the hook I had been willing to put myself on for her for all those years in the mistaken belief that this was what she wanted and needed. It gave me the confidence to believe that I was entitled to be the centre of my own life and that it was OK to say no. It contributed in no small measure to the fact that I now haven't seen my daughter or grandchildren since December 28th 2012.

I could tell you what happened but those reasons have little to do with why it actually happened. In my gut I feel that for both of us somehow the die was cast in that first year. Our relationship feels more archetypal than personal, almost as though we are both condemned to sift through the feelings and actions and reactions we generate in each other, saying "Is this yours or mine?" "And this, is this mine or yours or someone else's?" It breaks my heart to see her crave closeness and comfort but to sow discontent and loneliness. Distance is now the gift I give her – distance and love. Love always, not from guilt but from necessity. I am not me if I do not love her.

And here it is, the love I have been trying to extend to my daughter through all the difficult years, the love that is still here. It has been through the fire and tested; it no longer requires her to see it or feel it for me not to doubt its scimitar point as it rends me through again. I have been broken by my love for her: broken apart, flattened, disassembled and reassembled. It is in this love that I trust that this is not the end of our story, but that if it is, it will be because it is her decision and that has to be a good thing if I truly love her.

To blame her for seeing through me right from the start, for finding me not enough would add yet another layer of pain to the ache of being seen through and not being enough for the one who has taught me many of the most important lessons in my life, and I will not do it. After all, she is my darling, my first born, my lovely girl, my wayfarer, my compass, my brave one and she always will be.

Chapter Seven – Sharon

I seemed to spend most of my childhood wishing I'd been adopted. In my waking fantasies, a letter would arrive one day telling us all that my 'real' parents wanted me back. All would be well. I would finally be happy. Thanking the people I lived with for looking after me, I would wave goodbye as I went to be with the people that loved me and wanted me.

My sister was theirs, sure enough. Upon her head was bestowed limitless affection, affirmation and love. She couldn't really do anything wrong, it seemed. I couldn't work it out – I couldn't understand how my mother's attitude towards us could be so completely different. She was cuddled, she was kissed, she sat on Mother's lap and had countless stories read to her, whilst I listened on from across the room. And I accepted this as my reality. After all, I didn't know any different. I assumed I was simply un-loveable.

Sometime later, in my early twenties and with a toddler in tow, my son's father's voice resounded in my head most days: "I try so hard, but you are just un-loveable." He liked me very much, he was good and kind and a brilliant father, but he was right. I was un-loveable and somehow, somewhere deep inside I knew it to be true. It always had been.

The end of this relationship set the pattern for the ones that followed. They all seemed to start with a tremendous love affair, level off after a while, then become unbearably difficult after not very long, with me ultimately realising yet again that I'd fallen for someone completely unavailable to me. It happened every time. Each time the unavailability became stronger. Perhaps it was I who was the unavailable one.

I blamed my partners. I always blamed the partners, until I reached my forties and reflected back after years of therapy and it all started to make sense. It wasn't their fault; I had always done the choosing. I'd run so far and so fast for some of them, I hadn't paused for breath to realise they weren't interested, or if they were, they weren't able to return any real affection. But it didn't seem to matter. The more unavailable they were, the more I had to be with them. Some of them were substance abusers: drug users and alcoholics, and still I chased them and hunted them down. Most of them had had an abusive childhood, like I thought I'd had and it appeared to me to be such a meeting of minds, such a unification of experiences, that the idea of not being in a relationship with such and such a man (or woman) was abhorrent.

Some of them were emotional abusers and with them I felt safe. I felt as though things were how they were meant to be. Nowadays I recoil in horror at the memory of these experiences, or when I see a friend experiencing something similar. But at the time it made absolute sense, even though I didn't know why. It felt right, to feel like that: worried and anxious all the time.

My mother was difficult to live with. She resented my presence from the outset and I think I was always aware of that. She fell pregnant fairly young, at the age of 21, at the time when she was leading a very glamorous life in London, in the swinging sixties, with a very exciting job, loving her life. Her pregnancy was to change all of that. She had to move back to her small provincial town in Devon, pregnant, to marry a man she didn't love, didn't want to be with and who had simply been a passing drunken fling. She left her best friend behind in London and could only stand back and watch from afar the lifestyle she would have had.

She and my father moved into a very small flat and became penniless, destitute almost. There was no money in either family and they lived on virtually nothing, whilst my father spent long days and weeks away at a training college. There was no help from my bitter grandmother, angry with my mother for losing all those glittering opportunities. And into this scenario I arrived into the world. A bonny baby, according to photographs, but not the boy hoped for by my parents, grandparents, uncles, cousins and aunts. We moved into another flat in a large shared house. My bedroom was next to the stairs and, as I was young, there was no lock on the door. I do recall having nightly visits from one of the male tenants, but I don't recall any of the details. I was entrusted into his care frequently during the daytime, for my mother to have "a break" from me, and on one occasion the police were called because he didn't bring me back from the park in time. I did grow up with a morbid fear of that park, but I never knew why.

We moved when I was four, into our own house. My mother used to cry every night when my father was out; I used to hear her when I went to bed. Whatever I had experienced at the old flat had made me very insecure and every single night, without fail, I used to call down to my parents from my bed, to check if they were still there. My calling downstairs elicited a strange response. My father would storm up the stairs, wooden spoon in hand and beat me with it until I cried and then stopped crying. Night after night for as long as I could remember. Then my sister was born and it changed. My mother started to smile.

As I grew older, I became less happy. The wooden spoon didn't bother me any more (although it still appeared from time to time if I was "cheeky"). The memory of the nightly visits from the man didn't bother me. What really, really, really upset me was that whenever things went wrong for my mum, it was always my fault. Or so I was told. Then it became apparent that whenever anything went wrong for anyone, it was my fault. I lived my life in absolute morbid fear of my mum's dark moods. Moods would swing backwards and forwards without any provocation and it was always my fault. I lived my life with a knot in my stomach. I felt sick most of the time. I would get breathless; I would dread coming home. This is what emotional abuse feels like.

She would spend weeks on end in bed, ill, because of something I had done or something I had said, or hadn't done, or hadn't said. She told me she hated me, she wished I'd never been born, that I had ruined her life. I developed a stomach ulcer and a stammer and later, a nervous tic. I stopped coming home, finding happiness in the homes of friends instead whenever I could. I became a teenager and wild resentfulness kicked in. But still I lived in fear of upsetting people. By now my mother was spending so much time in bed, I had become a young carer. My life revolved around trying not to upset her. And then I started to hate her. I moved out as soon as possible.

On a bright Tuesday afternoon a couple of years later, I returned from university to my shared house to some shocking, terrible news. My housemate had just found out her parents had both been killed in a traffic accident and was, understandably, devastated. I was shocked and horrified by my own reaction.

I wished it had happened to me.

And then I had to live with the guilt of my reaction. So followed decades of abusive relationships. I chose co-dependency in most of my relationships. I chose emotional unavailability in all of them. I had children with some of them. None of them worked. I worked hard throughout because I needed to depend upon myself. I looked after them most of the time. I had no security, no help, no love and no comfort from them. I was repeating history.

As the years went by, my mother and I slowly grew closer, bit by tiny bit. My anger and hatred towards her gradually began to dissipate until one June day, prompted by my therapist, I asked my mother why she had always shown so much love and affection towards my sister, but none for me. Her answer was a revelation.

"I don't really know why, but I found I couldn't really bond with you as a baby. I didn't want to pick you up, I felt repulsed by breast-feeding and I couldn't cuddle you. I resented you being in my life. I couldn't help the way I felt. I felt unhappy for years and years, until another baby came along. I think nowadays they would call it post-natal depression."

So there it was: my answer. That simple. My jaw could have hit the floor. I realised that every unhappiness I had experienced as a child was the result of my mother trying to bring up a small child whilst suffering from depression. We hadn't bonded, we hadn't experienced that essential emotional longing and belonging that a love between a mother and baby should bring. The feeling of togetherness, the bond so powerful that I still have, thankfully, with my own grown-up children. I was a baby alone in the world. The world was cold, I was hungry and my needs weren't being met. I was unloved.

As a small child, needing my family, I didn't learn how to be loved. I couldn't expect it, then, as an adult. I didn't want it, I didn't know how to accept it, I certainly didn't need it. After all, if I had managed without it as a baby, I certainly wasn't going to need it later. Little wonder that I rebelled later, against life. I abused drugs, alcohol, myself. I self-harmed, got in trouble with the law and chose abusive relationships.

I have lived alone for a few years now, unable to trust my own judgement in a potential partner. I love my children so very much and am utterly thankful every day that the cycle didn't continue. I am lucky to have bonded strongly with them. I am closer to my mum now that I understand. I only wish she could have had the help she so badly needed to have been a normal mum. How very different my life would have been.

Chapter Eight – Lottie

It feels like a real challenge to tell you about my experiences of motherhood. Although my daughter is nearly 14 I rarely think of myself as a mother. I am 'the parent', just as responsible for putting up shelves and changing fuses as I am for the emotional nurturing and preparing the meals for Sophie. For as long as I can remember I have been all parenting roles rolled into one, and yet there was a time when there was two of us, and that is when I connect with the title of mother most, even though my experiences were unusual.

In 1999 I was living with my partner, Dudley. Our lives were nothing out of the norm. We had done well for ourselves. Both still in our twenties, we lived in a nice house and went on nice holidays, and while the rest of the world was eagerly anticipating the new millennium, we were awaiting the birth of our first child. In the October, when I was five months pregnant, we were lucky enough to get the opportunity to go to New York for a few days, and on reflection it is always to this trip that I can pinpoint a change in our relationship. I got flu and, to be honest, I made it a miserable trip for everyone else involved. I had my first experience of buying baby clothes and for me, during our time away something invisible and yet very real switched in our relationship.

Two nights after returning from our trip I awoke in the middle of the night to find Dudley's elbow in my stomach. I assumed he was moving around in his sleep and gave him a shove to the other side of the bed. He was not asleep, and it was not an accident. Instead it was the beginning of a physical assault that lasted three hours and resulted in me needing to visit the hospital for treatment for myself and my unborn child. I think shock prevented me from reacting quickly enough to what had happened, and before I knew it lies had been put in place to cover things up. I was numb, at least emotionally. Promises were made about attending therapy, about it never happening again, and how things would be made up for. I was now expecting the child of an abuser.

There were no more physical assaults before Sophie was born, but Dudley's promises were soon broken, and I regularly suffered verbal abuse that felt like it had no rhyme nor reason. One morning he would wake up, look at me and give me a kiss on the forehead; the next morning he would gaze over and say "What are you looking at, you f**king c**t?" I could literally taste both the fear and the anger within my home, and regularly took the dog out for long walks when I wasn't at work to escape, even though I was getting increasingly heavier and larger. My experience seemed so far removed from anything that I had learnt about domestic abuse that I didn't really know what to do.

Alongside that there were Dudley's constant threats about what he would do if I shared what I was experiencing with anyone. I felt trapped, and my feelings of responsibility to provide for my unborn child led me to stay on in the relationship.

On 15th February 2000 my daughter popped into my life – quite literally! A condition running in the family known as expulsive labour meant that, although I'd had a natural birth, I needed to be taken off for an epidural straight after Sophie arrived. It would be fair to say that my maternal instinct did not kick in immediately, and as I was being wheeled out of the room I looked over and saw my daughter lying on her father's chest, and my over-riding thoughts were that I'd quite like to bleed until I ceased to be, that I'd like to leave the two of them to it to see how they got on, that I did not want to be a part of their existence any more. These thoughts did not last for long.

After my procedure I was taken onto a ward and Sophie was placed next to me, and within minutes I became 100% grounded in being a mother. I knew that I would do whatever it took to protect my little girl and provide for her. Sadly, at that time, the only way I could see of doing that was to surrender everything I needed for my own protection and survival.

The emotional trauma of what I was experiencing took its toll on me physically too, and ten days after giving birth I weighed only 7 stones, and I continued to lose weight on an ongoing basis. In the meantime, abuse from Dudley grew, and verbal onslaughts followed me everywhere I went. I started off breast-feeding Sophie, and I was good at it; it was something that came naturally to me and I enjoyed it, but Dudley had different ideas. As the weeks progressed my feeding experience turned into a nightmare, with my over-riding memories of breast-feeding now being of carrying my daughter from room to room as Dudley followed us around the house with perpetual verbal taunts and abuse. Regularly I would have big fat tears rolling down my face, and I can still see them splashing onto Sophie's beautiful baby face. After around six weeks I became unable to feed her properly myself, as I knew what to anticipate if I tried to do so while he was in the house. The name calling and unending mockery had become too much for me, and although I initially tried to mix breast and bottle feeds, by two months after her birth Sophie was being fed by bottle alone.

I would like to say that not all days were bad, but I cannot recall any good ones. Sometimes Dudley would get up with Sophie on a weekend morning saying that he would look after her, but he did not. He would sit her on his lap in front of the TV while he played on the Playstation, regularly not bothering to change her nappy or feed her. I could not bear to stay in bed and see her left like this for hours, and so more and more verbal abuse was rolled out in my direction, for interfering and not allowing him to have time with his daughter.

I now know that by the time I returned to work, most of my family believed I was suffering with post-natal depression. Going back to work terrified me. I was a residential social worker, working shifts. As Dudley worked flexi-time the idea had always been for me to initially work the odd evening or weekend shift while he looked after the baby. I was going to have to leave Sophie with Dudley. I was scared.

It very quickly became apparent that when I did go to work Sophie was not looked after. Certainly for early shifts starting at 7am it was obvious that she was left in her cot for hours, while Dudley had his morning lie in, and when I was on a late shift during the week, he took her and left her at his mum's while he went to the pub. I'm sure it should have been an easier decision for me to make, but coming to the conclusion that I would not be able to work anymore was heart-breaking. Although every inch of my maternal instinct wanted to keep Sophie safe and well looked after, surrendering my one piece of freedom and individuality was oh so very hard. Also, by this time Dudley controlled pretty much everything within the relationship. Letting go of my own ability to earn money gave him full financial control too, and from that moment on there seemed to be no turning back from the precipice I felt I was on the edge of.

When Sophie was around six months old she was diagnosed with a heart murmur, and it was the hospital appointment in relation to this that led to the next large physical assault. A 'silly' argument in the car on the way home initially gave Dudley an excuse to lock me out of the house with Sophie; he also took my bank cards and cut them up. When he eventually let me in, it began. In a two and a half hour assault he injured my shoulder, held scissors to my throat and left me literally fearing for my life. In the end I phoned my sister, who came with her husband, helped remove mine and Sophie's basic essentials and took me to my parents' house 40 miles away, where we stayed in my parents' spare bedroom for nearly two months.

Hindsight is a wonderful thing, and if I'd have had it at the time I would never have stepped foot in my house again, or spoken even a word to Dudley, but I did not have the benefit of what I know now, and slowly but surely I began seeing him more, and being fed his false promises once again. I was also too scared to tell my parents what I had been experiencing. My own motherhood had made me acutely aware of the emotional pain you experience when someone harms your child. I did not want to put my own mother and father through that. It appeared to be too late to turn back.

From almost the day I returned to the house with Sophie I regretted it. The apprehension and fear there had become palpable to me in equal measures. Dudley controlled everything, and went out of his way to make life miserable in every way possible. He was furious that I had involved my family in his own private reign of terror, and vowed to kill me if I ever involved them in our relationship again. I believed him. I promised him I would not. I promised myself that if he physically assaulted me again I would call the police, not my sister. I kept my promises; he did not.

From then on every day literally seemed like a living nightmare where I was verbally, emotionally, psychologically and financially abused, whilst struggling to provide care for my daughter throughout her formative months. I didn't go out of the house unless I absolutely had to, and the dog became Sophie's best, and probably only, friend.

Then one day, coming close to Christmas, there was a conversation that made me come to at least a little bit of my senses. When Dudley came home from work you could almost taste the tension in the air that surrounded him. One of the first things he asked was "Have you been to the shops today?" and when I replied we'd been to Tesco he let rip with yet another barrage of abuse about how I'd been going out spending his money. Who did I think I was? But I had a 'penny drops' moment when I realised that there had been no right answer to the question. Had I answered that we had not been to the shops I would have still received the verbal onslaught, this time for not going out to get the food that we needed. I suddenly knew with certainty that I could never make this right, that I needed to get myself, and my daughter, out of this, but I also truly believed he would never let us go.

Dudley was due to be going to a conference in America in April. I started hoarding anything and everything I could so that we would be able to run away while he was gone. I had a growing awareness of the fact that my daughter was nearly a year old and was witnessing everything that went on. Increasingly she would not move away from my side, and I was conscious of the fact that my lack of self-esteem was rubbing off on her every day. Without telling Dudley my plans, I also started openly telling him that I did not want to stay with him anymore, and this had a strange effect. Incredulously, he seemed genuinely upset that I did not want to be with him anymore. He constantly threatened me with homelessness and court battles for Sophie if I should leave, but he also appeared to have moments where he was filled with remorse for what he had done. He appeared to believe that I was a big part of the problem between us, but he also seemed to recognise that the only solution was for us to be apart.

At the beginning of March 2001, just a couple of weeks after Sophie's first birthday, this depressive remorse seemed to get the better of him, and he agreed to leave. In my heart I knew that this would only be a temporary thing, but it felt like a massive relief and a prayer answered. After discussion with his parents, where nothing was admitted to, he packed his bags and went to stay with them.

The peace and freedom of no Dudley lasted one week and one day. On the Sunday evening, after Sophie had gone to bed, he returned to the house. The physical and sexual assault lasted three hours. I had never experienced such fear before, and then I was left with a crippling decision. Dudley marched downstairs screaming "See what I can do, see what I can do," and left me in the bedroom next to the room Sophie was in. I was physically shaking so much that I was unable to get my clothes back on properly, and my legs were literally weak underneath me. I knew that if I took the opportunity to get out I would have to leave Sophie.

It wasn't until I was sitting in the car with the door locked behind me that I realised I didn't even have any shoes on.

How I composed myself enough to drive I will never know, but when I arrived at my sister's house I knew exactly what I had to do. I called the police, and in turn they went to rescue my little girl. I had to go to the hospital for medical treatment, but I was told that Dudley had locked himself in with her and the police had had to kick down the door.

Sophie was returned to me the next morning and from then on my role as a mother ended, and I became the parent I am today. We will never truly know what triggered Dudley's behaviour; I have been told that he exhibits psychopathic tendencies that is all. I do know that although it has been an incredibly tough journey, those months of troubled beginnings have made Sophie and me strong together beyond imagination, enabling me to be

100% the parent, and her to bloom and flourish into her teenage years.

Chapter Nine – Anne-Marie

At 1.15pm on the 20th July 2013, an unrecognised number appeared on my mobile phone screen and a stranger said, *"Your daughter is gravely ill and we're trying to save her life."* It had, up until that point, been an ordinary sunny Saturday morning. I got up early and went out to do some chores. A little bit later Martha, my 15 year old daughter, dragged herself out of bed and cycled to Kayaking Club as she did every Saturday.

What unfolded after kayaking is that she allegedly swallowed half a gram of white powder at 11.30am which we now know was MDMA (more widely known as ecstasy). She collapsed at 1.15pm and never regained consciousness. She died officially at 2.17pm, and her death is still being investigated.

I started to write within a few hours of her death as I needed to channel the extraordinary pain. Despite being heavily sedated at the time, I've never been so focused and driven to write as I did in the moments and weeks that followed my only child's death. This is an extract from Day 2:

My eyelids finally stopped fighting the sleep last night and I slept deeply and soundly. I wake up early. My heart is beating, but it pangs with the loss, knowing that I will always miss her. I missed her even when she was only away for a few hours, but this type of 'missing' is peculiar, unnatural. Getting used to her not being here goes against what every cell in my body feels. I am a mother; that is what I do.

Mothers care and plan ahead, mothers nurture and nag you to tidy your bedroom. Mothers tell you to shower after you've been swimming in the lake. Martha would make excuses and go to bed with the grit of the day on her. I'll never get to nag her again, I'll never get to tell her that her room is a mess ... oh how I wish I could nag her again and hear her excuses ... "I'll do it later, I'll shower after kayaking tomorrow." I'd be both bemused and irritated by this, but that is a luxury now that I'll never get to practise again. I am still a mother, but not a practising one. I have all these mothering skills which I know will always be useful in my life, but their original purpose is no longer what they'll be used for.

So I did what I needed to do today, I went online and started looking at coffins: what would she like, what would Martha choose? She was far from traditional but she wouldn't want anything gimmicky either. The answers come to me gently. I know that whatever is chosen, it'll be lovely and really, does it matter that much? The true meaning of life has hit me like a bolt of lightning and the previous version of me now seems trivial – but it's tragic that this had to happen in order for this stoic version of myself to surface.

I'm going through her clothes today, to choose an outfit to dress her in. She liked to wear crop tops and denim shorts that were more revealing than any parent is comfortable with. "Pull those shorts down," I hear the previous version of myself say. Today I say, "Martha, what would you like me to dress you in – what outfit is the right one to represent you for the very last time?" It definitely won't be denim shorts and a crop top, but it'll be something that'll show my precious daughter off beautifully.

Martha, if you are with me now, please hold my hand and guide me to show me what you want. I love you so much and don't know where to channel this love now. I have too much of it and it was all for you. I'll give some to myself now as I need it; I'll give some to family, friends and strangers, but I've still got too much left. It feels like a burden, but I know it'll get easier.

Nearly six months on, my new life is taking shape; I'm getting used to it just being me. There's an incredible simplicity about my life now. A pint of milk goes down at a mere inch every couple of days, whereas before, Martha would come into the living room looking delirious and out of breath from downing her favourite drink. "We need more milk," she'd say, as she wiped away the milky moustache.

Surprisingly though, I'm actually enjoying my new-found independence – I don't have a choice but to get on with things, so I do. I'm seeing Oxford with fresh eyes and exploring it without the worry of what Martha wants for dinner, or whether she'll be in a good mood after school.

I've never respected life like I do now. I look around at the world with wonderment and realise how distracted I was before all this happened. Without the distractions that being a practising mother brings I notice things I've never noticed, such as the faint figures of elderly people as they idle along the pavement, each step carefully considered, and little babies that stare at me as though they know something. Their gummy smiles shine from their prams and fill my heart with a little bit of joy that only those very simple and precious moments can bring.

I experience great joy from being around other people's children. Although I've always loved children I have more time and patience for them now without the distraction of my own. I used to have one eye on my mobile phone looking out for a text from Martha, rather than being really present in the room – *Does my girl need to reach me?* I'd worry.

My friends 'visit Martha' at her grave and I jokingly ask how she was; they play along with me and say she was fine - this makes me feel like a practising mother again. I am still able to laugh and feel great joy as that is who I am and I really think I deserve to be happy, especially now. I no longer take any fragment of happiness for granted; I am utterly grateful for any relief from the pain and anguish, so I relish it, breathe it in and hold onto it until the moment passes. "Farewell my friend," I think, "see you again soon, I hope," and happiness closes the door saying it'll call by again soon.

When I visit Martha's grave, I don't feel anything as the plot only symbolises where she was laid to rest, not who she was. She saw the world like nobody else I've ever met. She'd walk her three-legged rabbit, Bluebell, on a lead around our local streets, much to the bemusement of strangers – but to anyone who knew her, that was just what Martha was like: quirky, interesting, with an incredibly sharp wit.

It had been just the two of us since she was ten months old, so we were incredibly close. When we held hands it was so familiar to me that it was as though I was holding my own. So losing her was like my own leg being amputated, making me unsteady on my feet, having to get over the shock and reacclimatise to my new circumstances. The pain in my heart was so acute that I went to the doctor, who prescribed me with indigestion tablets. *I don't have indigestion,* I'd think, but there's nothing that they can prescribe for a broken heart, apart from time passing and doing whatever it takes to find your own way to heal.

The day before Martha died I uncharacteristically took her out of school as she was exhausted from studying for her exams. I picked up Martha's boyfriend and we were on Sandbanks beach by 9am. I found a spot, plonked myself down and panned left to right over the misty distant landscape. The sea was glistening, the seagulls were dancing majestically in the sky and I slowly breathed in the beautiful day ahead. It was perfect, just what we needed.

I'm still a mother – I'll always be a mother – but I've forced myself to be incredibly practical and accept how things are. When I came home from the hospital immediately after she died, I went into the bathroom and threw her toothbrush in the bin. I didn't want to live in a museum or have a daily reminder every morning when I saw her toothbrush next to mine. So my toothbrush stands alone, as do I.

Whenever I want to be with my girl now, I just close my eyes and am back at the beach momentarily and she's happily sitting beside me. The tide comes in and the impression she made in the sand is washed away, but I know it was there, but a moment ago.

Anne-Marie Cockburn
Author of "5,742 Days"

Chapter Ten – Nicky

Looking back as an adult I class my childhood as idyllic. I had two parents who loved me, supported me, laughed with me and gave me good guidelines. My dad had his own business, but always had time to talk to my brother and me. He worked hard and saw himself as our provider, but would still be there to enjoy the laughter, the holidays and the outings that are etched into my memory.

My mum was and still is the most loving, caring and compassionate human being I know. Our care was very tactile, with endless smiles, kisses goodbye and goodnight hugs. Our clothes were always immaculate and my brother and I always looked smart. I later learned that this sometimes involved staying up past midnight washing and drying our favourite outfits as money was tight.

From the doting mother of a toddler to the sympathetic ear for a teenager, my development in early life was cared for and tended by one amazing lady. Even during those petulant teenage years I always knew I was loved.

Perhaps I was wearing rose-tinted spectacles about what family life was, but my school friends had similar experiences and so I never questioned whether this was the exception rather than the rule. As I grew older I decided this was what my family life would be like… and for a while it was.

I met my future husband just as I was leaving school. We started dating and very soon my parents realised that this relationship was more serious. It wasn't long before we were together every day, switching between each other's houses but constantly hand in hand. Apparently we were 'courting' – this was how we were labelled in the family.

The progression from going out together to being engaged and entering into married life seemed natural to me. I don't think I ever really sat down and consciously thought about whether I had other options. I knew I was in love, I knew I wanted to settle down and start a family and I knew my boyfriend loved me. We had talked about children and agreed we wanted two or three. Our conversations were straightforward and innocent, in the way of two teenagers with a lot of growing up to do who already considered themselves to be grown-ups!

From the minute I found out I was pregnant with our first baby I felt wrapped in a warm bubble that was a mix of love, anticipation, excitement and completion. The morning sickness was unpleasant and to this day I remember the tired and constant nausea! Finding out that cherries were the solution was amusing; I loved how Mother Nature took over and I watched in awe as my body adapted to carry this little human being growing inside.

Our families were delighted at the news and lots of excited talk ensued; would it be a boy or a girl? Who would they look like? How soon could the grandparents step in and babysit?

I will never forget the night my daughter arrived. As they placed her on my chest I cannot describe the wonder and love that I felt. My little miracle was here, perfect and beautiful. My husband was as overwhelmed as I was when his firstborn was placed in his arms and there were many tears of joy. The next day I listened, laughing and with tears in my eyes, as he described dancing in the street and celebrating becoming a daddy to a beautiful daughter.

Family life really was as I had imagined and I took to motherhood like a duck to water. I nurtured our daughter, nurtured our home and worked two days a week. Money was tight and there were a few quarrels, but we always found we could do the important things and looking back we didn't really want for anything. There was a lot of time spent as a family, where we shared looking after our daughter equally. A special link grew between dad and daughter and I clearly remember looking on at the shared jokes, the giggles and the play wrestling with a contented smile on my face.

When I discovered I was pregnant again the excited flutter arose once more. Baby number two was fascinating to my daughter. She would poke and cuddle my growing tummy and point and say, "Baby!" with a big grin. Again the boy or girl conversation was bandied around; I was carrying very differently so many people voted for a boy this time. Initially I thought another girl was on her way, but as the pregnancy continued I did start to change my mind. "As long as he or she has all of their fingers and toes I'll be happy!" became my phrase of choice.

It turned out this really was a different pregnancy – all 45 weeks of it! Our second born was in no rush to come into this world and week after week I would visit my midwife to be told, "Things are happening, any minute now, honestly!" I tried all the home remedies to induce the birth, from hot baths and burning curries to invigorating walks and the most disgusting and dreaded castor oil. Nothing, it seemed, would encourage this baby to make its entrance.

Imagine my excitement and relief at five weeks overdue when proper labour started. I waddled my way from my mum's front door to the car, panicking that I had left it too late as my labour became intense so quickly.

We arrived at the hospital and were just about to be given a bed when everyone realised that now this baby had made up its mind it was coming fast! At 2.38am a pink and rosy-cheeked perfect baby girl made her way into the world. With a shock of blonde hair and huge, deep blue eyes my daughter looked at me with the most aware and intense gaze. I was in love.

The long wait, the intensity and the speed of my labour, mixed with the gas and air, seemed to be catching up with me and everything took on a surreal feeling after that. Having a bath and getting up to the ward were a bit of a drug-hazed, tired blur, but by the time I was sitting up in bed with a cup of tea in my hand tucking into some toast my energy rallied. At that point my husband made his excuses and with hardly a word and a peck on the cheek he was gone.

I sat there trying to make sense of what had just happened. Last time the nurses had literally had to peel him away from the cot as he wanted to sit and dote all night. Had he really just left? What could possibly be happening? A wave of shock, angst and panic washed over me as I looked at my peaceful sleeping baby. No answers were forthcoming, but the exhaustion chose that moment to return and I thankfully drifted off to sleep.

The morning flew by as my mothering instinct surged to the fore and I set about working out what this baby actually needed. The extra five weeks in vitro had obviously done her the world of good as she was awake, alert and ready to play! She would look around the room with her wide eyes, seeming to take in every detail.

At visiting time her sister made a huge entrance, dashing in bubbling over with excitement, smiles and love. She was so gentle and so involved, taking her hand and introducing herself proudly as the big sister. It was a wonderful sight to behold and I quickly settled baby into toddler's arms with a bundle of blankets for extra padding and safety.

During this whole process the father of my children stood barely inside the curtain. After my third quizzical look and raised eyebrow he quietly uttered, "I wanted a boy."

The surreal quality of that moment strikes a chord even now. There I was with my two perfect, wonderful daughters sharing their first amazing meeting and my heart should've been bursting. Instead it had turned to a horrified, cold stone.

In that moment I wanted to shout and scream. I wanted to slap his face and wake him up to the fact that other people don't get this chance to be a father even once. Should I point out the miracle, the beauty and the gift of being able to share the lives of these two innocent souls? My skin crawled with the sickening magnitude that hit me with those four simple words and for what seemed like an eternity the world swam around me.

I chose to turn away silently and take the biggest breath of my life. I swallowed the panic, the anger, the fear and the enormity of this situation in one big, painful gulp. And then, without a look back or a second thought, I painted a big, fake smile on my face and turned my attention back to my beautiful and wonderful children.

That was it. I simply carried on with caressing and cuddling my children and planning the mammoth operation of getting home and settling in. It was easy to distract myself with the constant feeds and daily juggle of a toddler and a newborn. A few days later my husband quietly muttered that he was "Okay with it now." I murmured something about that being good and carried on.

I told no one. I became a totally absorbed, workaholic, utterly devoted, 24/7 mother. When I heard a cry in the night I was there in an instant; there was no sharing as I was successfully breastfeeding this time. I took on as much of the caring as possible without being obvious and my girls became my world. I socialised a bit, but preferred the sanctuary of being home alone.

During those early months shock number two arrived when my beloved grandfather died suddenly of a stroke. Everyone around me, including a very watchful health visitor, put my growing depression and ensuing illness down to this. Of course that was an easy assumption to make as I had deeply buried away my secret.

Day by day my relationship with my daughters grew as my relationship with my husband dwindled. How can you share your life with a man who has rejected the daughter you have given him? Growing inside of me was a strength, a steeliness and resilience that had so far lay dormant.

My idyllic view of the world had meant that I'd never needed to call on it before, but now I needed it and there it was.

That resilience saw me through my divorce eight years later. It saw me through the fear, the outbursts, the pain and the panic. Through the tears of children who didn't know why this was happening, that threatened to wash me away with grief. Eventually their father told them the story of the rejection and they realised why I had left him. Sadly this damaged their relationship with him, something I would not have wished for. It did, however, give them an understanding of my reasons and my relationship with my daughters deepened still further.

So what have I learned? I have learned that human beings are a constant source of surprise. That you can think you know someone and then one day in an instant realise that you don't. I have learned that the mothering instinct can be so strong it can carry you through experiences that you thought were impossible. The inner lioness can sleep peacefully until her children are threatened, when she will rear her head with a roar and carry herself and her offspring to safety with lightning speed and grace.

I have learned that when you unwaveringly and unconditionally love your children and focus on the positive, life has a way of giving you support in the strangest of ways. It may feel like you are frozen to the spot and unable to take a step, but by taking a breath you can choose to do one thing. This can then lead to a sequence of synchronistic events and chance encounters with people who will change your life.

I remember with clarity and force of emotion the fear of rocking the boat, worried about the upheaval and the changes that my children would face. By trying my best, reaching out for help when I needed it and always being open to another way I have brought in a peace and happiness that makes my heart sing. Through my work I get to inspire others to take their first step for a better life.

But for me, what brings a huge smile to my face is the knowledge that my daughters, now twenty-two and twenty, have myriad happy memories that have overtaken those early years. They are rounded, intelligent, positive thinking individuals who travel the globe, make good choices and experience life in a mostly fearless way. They adapt to changes well, always expect good things to happen and hold out for the things that they deserve. The relationship that we all share makes my heart swell with love and the laugh-'til-you-cry experiences that we regularly share are priceless.

Nicky Marshall
www.discoveryourbounce.co.uk

Chapter Eleven – Freya

Smooth cold manicured fingers and little wooden hugs

My story is kind of a love story. It follows the love/hate relationship I had with my mother as a small child; both of us stubborn and hot tempered and unable to break through the barriers we had built up. I tell the story using a series of poems that helped me to come to terms with my past.

This first poem is a very early childhood memory. I was maybe seven or eight years old and we were on a family walk: me, Mum, Dad and my little sister and brother. I had been dawdling and when I caught up I reached out to take Mum's hand in mine and she pushed me away.

Manicured fingers

The little girl with the mousy hair

reached out her hand.

A shy tentative yearning.

There was no one.

The smooth cold manicured fingers

shrugged out of reach.

Like grasping branches

in an angry wind.

The unkind words, dropped thoughtlessly,

At longing little feet.

Only searching for comfort

In her mother's embrace.

The adult fuelling fury

The teenage rage unleashed.

So many dreams forgotten,

Love withered unsaid.

It was too late for holding hands

Too many years had passed

The cold wind swirled full;

Haunted with questions unasked

The wooden hugs now years too late

The past forever stained.

The unkind words she had let go.

The little girl remained.

I remember this happening like it was yesterday, seeing her instinctively recoil at my touch. I remember thinking if she didn't want to hold my hand I would never try to hold hers again. I held my head up high and walked tall and straight with my hands deep in my pockets, not looking at her, this woman, this stranger, my mother.

I used to watch her with her smooth cold beauty and perfect sculpted manicured fingernails and longed for the cuddle that never came; all that came was the order to 'stop staring'. I was a prickly child with bad eczema and maybe I pushed her away too, I don't remember. What I remember is a house thick with quietly boiling anger, tension and cruelty; unkind words said in the heat of an argument that can never be unsaid. These memories are sad, shrivelled, nasty things that lodge in my heart like thorns. These feelings were compounded as I watched my little sister effortlessly receiving all the cuddles and praise I longed for. I could see my mum loved my little sister. She was the favourite. My perfect little sister who could do no wrong – and I hated them both more and more each day. I was a bit of a tomboy so I got on well with my brother and I am ashamed to say we tormented my sister and left her out of our games, partly because she was different – she was special and we were not –but also because she was rubbish at ball games and football and preferred to be inside making things, reading or just being with Mum.

There are photos of me as a small baby cradled in her arms. In these photos she is pretty and blissfully happy but I don't remember the woman in these photos.

Who is she – this woman, my mother?

My mother was a very unhappy woman. She and my father married on the rebound and perhaps against the better judgement of friends and family, who cautioned rushing into anything. They met at church where my father was very much involved in teaching but Mum soon stopped going. I never found out why but when both partners have very different religious beliefs it doesn't help. It was a toxic and unhappy marriage. This is probably an understatement. They shared a bed but rarely spoke to one another. There was no affection from my mother; she pushed my father away. If they did speak it was to argue. When I consider that now, I cannot imagine how they did that. How they kept that up, how they ever got a good night's sleep. I think it explains why still to this day I cannot bear any tension and am hypersensitive to conflict or friction, even imagining it where there is none.

Dad tried to rectify this situation but his efforts fell on deaf ears. Watching this endless heartache and betrayal of their lost love was painful and depressing and made me hate her even more. But my mum was so unhappy and miserable. I wonder now if she was suffering with depression but with no one to speak to and trapped in a destructive marriage, all she could do was cling on and hope for escape. She despised my dad and it seemed she could see no way out of this situation, especially once the first little girl came along to cement the marriage in place. That little girl was me.

I was also a daddy's girl, perhaps more so since my mum seemed unable to show me any kindness, affection or love. My father more than made up for this. He showered us all with love, read us stories; our toys came to life and all had different voices and we knew, every second of every day, that he loved us. He never had a cross word except when we were really naughty, which was not often. I am forever thankful for this. Without him and also many kind friends and family who showered me with affection to make up for the lost mothering, what would have become of me?

My father was not without blame in this story. He allowed this unfair treatment and cruelty to continue under his nose. He never stood up for me in front of Mum. He also shared intimacies with me that a small child should never know. A little girl does not ever need to know that her mum only allowed sexual relations three times, which gave them three beautiful children. She does not need to know about all her father's secrets and longings. It was too much and, in its own way, destructive also.

This next poem explores my feelings about these shared intimacies.

Longing

Flattering the attention

Showered on the lonely girl

Where one failed to nurture

The other tried to mend.

He needed her ear to listen

Her kind words to soothe

Confided in her his longing

She didn't want this truth.

She only wanted comfort

Not boundaries to the wind.

Not such a special confidante

Just a father and friend.

He could not fix the woman

The bond tangled up and toxic.

So he told the little girl,

She was so special.

He shared his secrets and desires,

Dark failings and regrets.

But these adult conversations

cloaked the small girl's dreams.

It was flattering to have this very close relationship with my father, but he over-stepped the boundaries of what should be shared with a child, of any age. I still don't want to know this stuff as an adult and for the first time this year I have asked him to stop talking to me about private things. It is none of my business. My mother never ever spoke about anything private, and when they eventually got divorced I gained a new respect for her as she never tried to get us to take sides or shared anything inappropriate.

Seeing me so close to my father must have hurt my mother. I hurled insults at her. I told her I hated her, often. I am not proud of this but I was a child and I had no other way of getting her attention. I had a special look just for her: an unblinking hard long stare that spat hatred. It was my only weapon against her and she hated it. I feel intense guilt about this too. I cannot imagine being so cruel to anyone now, least of all my own mother, but these were small victories and they pleased me. How could I have been so cruel? But I was just a child and I was learning from the cold Ice Queen herself. All it would have taken was a warm smile, an apology, a kind word, an easy embrace; it was the little things that were missing. I didn't know how to make her love me so I strove to give her every reason to really hate me.

I held onto the dark secret that my mum didn't love me and I have no memories of cuddling my mum or being held, or comforted or kissed or playing games or doing anything, just my mum and me. But I do remember coldly the injustice of seeing my sister cuddled and hugged. The middle sister – the favoured one, yet I could do nothing right. My lifelong ambition then became to get her into trouble but my sweet, gentle little sister was never bad, she was just adorable and good and perfect. I hated her for that too but despite all this we were very close, holding our jealousy closer still; me jealous of her easy relationship with Mum and her jealous of my confidence, my freedom and my strength.

I was horrible to my mother but I was responding to her and learning from her. She shouted at me, I shouted back. She was unfair to me; she lost my respect. I thought I hated her and told her so but really it was fury, anger and deep, deep pain that she couldn't love me for who I was. She often used to say, "I wish you were more like your friend Caroline. I bet she's never rude to her mother." The years of slow mental rejection eroded what little respect was left from my childhood. There was never anything positive, no praise; she never said she loved me or was proud of me. I was too ashamed to speak about any of the things my mother said to me so I lied; to the outside world I created another mother. One who did love me, which leads to my third poem.

I lied...

I lied about the other day

It wasn't quite like that.

I did it so you might assume

She loved me.

I lied to make you like me.

So you wouldn't think me bad.

To hide my secret shame;

She didn't love me.

I lied about the little things;

The special kindnesses.

The way she might have been,

If she had loved me.

The other main ambition of my childhood was to smooth things over between Mum and Dad. I couldn't understand why they didn't get on. Dad was kind and gentle and Mum was beautiful yet her beauty was lost behind cold, frigid barriers that no one could get through. My efforts to communicate between them were futile; it was a cruel game I should never have got involved with because I could never ever succeed in making our house a happy one. I couldn't see that and I felt the guilt of that failure, blaming myself somehow for their failed marriage. Once Mum said to me, "You trapped me in the marriage; you were a mistake. If I hadn't had you I wouldn't be trapped in this loveless marriage." Once was enough. It stayed with me, festering deep inside. My mum doesn't love me and it's my fault.

It seemed everyone else was content to live like this, in a house thick with tension, nasty back-handed comments, vicious jibes. Why did I take all this guilt, shame and pain onto my shoulders? Why didn't I just distance myself like my brother and sister did?

Despite all the pain and heartache and guilt I have worn throughout my childhood and carried with me into adulthood I can now see that my mum gave me what she could: a safe place, shelter, food and clothing. We have all grown up with strong morals and principles and a work-hard ethic and everything that happened in my life makes me who I am today.

I can see how unhappy Mum was, and as an adult I know how hard it is to function, to go on when you feel so low. I have had a few bouts of depression and eventually found help and time to heal. My mother never got any help, never admitted she was unhappy – instead she bottled it all inside but it was a pathetic imitation of the mother we all craved to have. A happy mother, a smiling mother, a kind mother – it is all I strive for in my life now. Not possessions and money; just to be happy and content.

Through counselling I have learnt that it's OK. That none of what happened to me as a child was my fault and that my mum does love me, and she did back then too; she just wasn't able to show it in the way I hoped and longed for.

The things I know about my mum are memories that other people have given me. My nana, my auntie and Mum's cousin all shared stories with me so that I could build a picture in my own head of who Mum was and why she was the way she was. When I asked my mum, "Who was your first boyfriend?" or "Who was your best friend?" the reply is simply, "I can't remember."

I sometimes wish that I could forget but instead I remember every unkind gesture, cruel word and shouted argument as if they were yesterday, and I am curled in bed crying myself to sleep. I remember what it felt like be that little girl.

It is a hard sad little memory that I carry with me, always deep in my pocket like a smooth pebble that I turn, smoothing it and warming it. But it is always cold and hard. Maybe one day soon I will have the courage to fling that stone back into the ceaseless churning swell of the ocean of life where it belongs. I don't want these dark memories any more; that tiny pebble weighs so heavily in my pocket and that is not who I want to be any more.

My aunt once told me, "I can't believe she is the same person. Your mum was always such a cold, distant, uncaring person when you were little and yet now she is completely different. She's transformed."

Now she is always happy, laughs easily, loves her own company, is independent and goes out walking. She has lots of friends. She adores all five of her grandchildren and has an easy loving relationship with them. She is kind and thoughtful and phones me regularly and she is one of the first people I would call for advice. She is my mother and she is proud of me. She even hugs me now: small little wooden hugs while patting me on the back. One day we will be on bear hug terms but it's alright because all that matters is that she is my mother and we love each other.

Chapter Twelve – Zed

"Mummy, which one is Michelle's hospital?"

I asked this innocent question one day when I was about two and a half, and it led to my recognising, for the first time, that I was different. Michelle was a friend and neighbour. I thought all children had 'a hospital'. My little sister and I had one each for different reasons - Great Ormond Street and Great Portland Street respectively. *"Michelle doesn't have a hospital,"* my mum explained. *"Why do I have a hospital?" "Because you're special."*

In my experience, the comparatively tiny group of us who have congenital deformities and abnormalities receive poorer treatment from the wider social group than those who acquire a disability later. I see it on the faces of people who ask questions. The 'There but for the grace of God go I' smile is replaced by nausea or fear sliding across their face. I sometimes wonder if they know that I see it. You are no longer someone they can relate to; you are now a freak. You are 'the other'. This is why I was not surprised when people found my journey into motherhood confusing and challenging.

I can't describe how damaging it is to be battered with the freak stick every day of your formative years. When I was eight, two boys held me against a classroom wall – a tiny little girl with half a leg, on crutches that day too. They told me I should have been drowned at birth. They produced a plastic supermarket bag from a pocket. One trapped me against the wall, the other pulled the bag over my head and held it round my neck; they laughed.

Whilst that particular attack was more dramatic than most, I suffered reactions born of the same feelings about my existence every day of my school life and often outside it too. It got worse at each school. I was stared at, pointed at, whispered about, walked around, shouted at, picked on, pushed and pulled, kicked and punched, humiliated and excluded. I felt so guilty about the pain and suffering that my disabilities caused my loving parents that I said nothing. I deserved this pain for turning up this way. My high school did me a huge disservice by not bothering to tackle it; quite the opposite more than once.

I needed and wanted to do some very considerable healing before entering motherhood. In my mid-twenties, I was still extremely damaged. I entered into and spent too long in an abusive relationship. With spinal surgery two years before still raw, my pain increased drastically rather than improved and with the addition of sore, debilitating conditions affecting my stump, I was often stuck on a sofa for weeks on synthetic morphine, which had deeply unpleasant side effects of sickness and sadness. This with a partner who inexplicably and rapidly leapt from joy and humour to terrifying anger. I wanted a child. I knew I had to do two things – get out of that relationship before I got broken and get some external input to my healing. After years of unpacking and analysing and gaining a real understanding about what had happened to me, I had got stuck. I couldn't find ways to stop being consumed with guilt and a gaping internal sadness. I wanted desperately to decrease the flashbacks and the following hours of distress I experienced whenever I was stared at.

I had CBT and found out that my negative baseline statement was 'I don't deserve to breathe'. Oh. I walked out on my partner, my home and my job in the space of two weeks. I worked on my head some more and then had over a year of psychotherapy. I learned how to re-frame more effectively. There was considerable surprise over how far I had got on my own and I really needed that boost to my self-esteem. I accepted that my head was going to be a lifetime's piece of work. During psychotherapy I had an epiphany. I realised that when people did a double take upon noticing my prosthesis, it made me feel like I had been caught out in a lie. After all these years from my first leg when I was five to now – trying to get a prosthesis that looks just like a leg. They don't look like legs; they can't. My solution was to commission some fantastic artwork and have it 'tattooed' into the prosthesis. Now when people stare, I have exercised some control over what is being stared at. I gave myself permission to lie when strangers ask invasive questions – I don't owe them my personal information. Recently, someone was treated to a very long and exciting tale about a hot air ballooning accident, which I described in an ebullient manner with lots of gesticulations. I have taken charge, and I make choices.

After years of healing, I still find being stared at difficult – and being stared at by children can trigger emotional flashbacks; I see a convex mirror with a multitude of jeering faces with greedy, spiteful eyes. I'm not looking forward to the years of collecting at the school gates. There will be bravery and tears. I will achieve some more healing as a result. I might have to seriously beef up my pirate tales!

"Yep. Cripples fuck too, you know."

I moved off with a small smile and a long release of breath that shivered tension from my shoulders. I wanted to shock her; I wanted her to stop and think. I was bone-weary of the same ignorant and invasive phrase spewed on me almost daily. Strangers and acquaintances, a lot of 'professional' people. All sorts of folk – split them into whatever groups you like, there was a squad in each subset.

"You did well to get pregnant with all your health problems."

Or just

"You did well to get pregnant."

Correlating mobility disabilities with poor health is like calling all mathematicians' probability theorists, but much more insulting. It's an illogical presumption, and yet a high proportion of people seem to hold it. Why are these people even thinking about my disabilities in this context? And what on earth has it got to do with them? Why would people believe that a missing limb guaranteed ill health, say a damaged heart or diabetes? Why would someone think that my failing spine and joints had made me infertile? Ludicrous ideas of 'the other'. Of course, we freaks are not quite human, so maybe we aren't sexual beings and even if we are, maybe we can't quite manage it. Poor freaks, what a shame.

No one tries to push me downstairs or suffocate me any longer, but strangers still point at me in the street and have even taken pictures. A woman once literally shielded her child from me, pulling him away. It's a virulent new virus – monopeditis! I expect his foot fell off around the corner. Sometimes I use a wheelchair and people hang their bags or lean on the handles, or wheel me out of the way in shops whilst I'm selecting produce.

According to some studies, the biggest reactions by a long way are triggered by seeing people with either missing limbs or facial disfigurements. I don't mind telling people about my stump; it is different and therefore fascinates some people. I do, however, object to complete strangers barrelling up to me, demanding *"What's wrong with your leg?"* without even making eye contact, let alone saying hello. I have some stock responses; my favourite is delivered in a bright conversational style: *"What's your bra size? Since we're playing 'swap personal questions with strangers'."* If one in ten of them stops and thinks, learns and grows, then I'll take the hit.

Watching people struggle with the idea of disability and motherhood was no surprise to me; I actually thought my pregnancy experiences of ignorance would be worse and had buffered myself for dealing with that. I was criticised, in varying manners and degrees of directness, but I didn't have energy spare to challenge false assumptions every time I saw them. Sometimes I could and people were always surprised; they didn't think you could have disabilities and high capability.

My pregnancy wasn't going to fit in a nice clean box and that was fine by me. While most mums-to-be wear slippers and buy shoes when their ankles suddenly blow up, I found that one morning I woke up unable to get into my leg. This fits in nicely with my sense of humour and provided a large number of pregnancy quips and quotes. The Leg Shop (prosthetics department at the hospital) cast and built me a new one in less than two weeks from my call to them, which is very impressive.

"But how are you going to manage?"

I doubt anyone really thinks this is actually a helpful question. *"Like I always do, thanks."* Piles of people seeing only problems and barriers. I just didn't see them. I came to motherhood not expecting to do things the same way that other people do them because that reflects my life experiences.

Parenting involves continuous change and there is a regular requirement to find solutions to existing problems as well as to negate future ones. I've been building up this sort of resourcefulness all my life. I am very used to swapping things around, re-organising, reconsidering, redesigning, adapting and doing things differently to other people. In this way, my physical differences have been a distinct advantage. Not for the first time in my life, my disabilities gave me a key set of experiences and knowledge that you can neither learn nor buy.

While many presume that my life is unpleasantly challenging I see lots of solutions, silver linings and benefits from my differences. I am not trying to say that there are no issues or barriers. There are hundreds; I just don't want to be trapped by them. I am bigger than them. Realising this was extraordinarily liberating, and a hard-won lesson. I'm also not saying that I am relentlessly cheerful. Some days I have to dig really deep to find the Zed that is bigger than the sum total of the challenges in front of me. Occasionally, I can't. I was a child when I decided that I didn't want to be miserable, give up, stop trying or accept limitations set by others. It's an easy choice to make, but not an easy choice to live with – but worth it.

I often see humour in my differences; it's been fantastic recently telling my now just-four pirate-obsessed son that I AM a pirate, just check out the leg! It's not a sadness to us. He has tried to wear my prosthesis a couple of times. He loves coming to the 'Leg Shop' and talks incessantly about what treat he will choose from the WRVS shop where I will also have the treat of a coffee. He loves my new leg, which has my dragon artwork re-tattooed, as he's only known the single colour purple prosthesis made in a hurry whilst I was pregnant. My son and I have fun with it – we've used my prosthesis as a cave entrance for little models or figures and laughed at how I can turn it back to front or use it like a croquet mallet with a ball. I take it off and shake it in the air like an old man with his walking stick, saying silly things in a ludicrous gruff voice. Sometimes, I subversively add monopeds into stories.

So how do the practicalities work? Creative and lateral thinking, largely. These are universal skills. Don't concentrate on what the problem is, concentrate on how you get to your end goal. Spend some time identifying what it is you are trying to achieve; it will also help articulate the stumbling blocks. Break it up into constituent parts of actions if need be and find your solutions step by step by re-framing, squinting, thinking and imagining. It can be a lot of fun, especially if you make the solutions amusing. Don't be afraid to try things out and don't listen to naysayers. I had a broad range of things that worked for me with a baby – some were about approach and attitude and some were practical ways of doing things or specific types of products. As a baby, Pip would sit and be held on my lap and we'd go "gaboomf" for every stair. We still do it sometimes for fun: "Can we go gaboomf please, Mummy?" Soft fabric baby slings in the house, co sleeping, strapping him to me in the wheelchair (he loved it), an evolving and adapting life. I am better than many able bodied people on the floor, as long as I take my leg off. I can scoot about on a tray-style plant stand on wheels. I targeted some teaching – Pip could get down the stairs with me next to him perfectly safely and independently very early. Dig deep, battle the pain and find the energy. Want to do it. Know what is safe.

I woke up every half hour when he was a baby, with a visceral need to check he was still alive. I knew it was statistically unlikely that he should die and he was perfectly healthy, but I had experiences that told me that babies do die, sometimes suddenly or inexplicably. He wouldn't let me put him down for the first sixteen weeks. I followed my instincts and his signals and we remained attached almost all the time and he was not asked to let go.

I was not about to complain, but it was hard and would have been much easier had I had some practical support in the house. Pip's dad was in the States. He came when our son was two weeks old, which was what I had suggested. He stayed for seven weeks before he had to go back to the other side of the pond. The next eleven weeks were the hardest. I remember once reaching into the fridge and breaking a chunk off a piece of cheese with one hand, whilst saying to him "If I don't eat then you won't eat." I was terrified of losing my milk. I was isolated. I adored my baby. I was overjoyed to have the privilege of motherhood. It was so intense the air became sticky. I felt so different that I was unable to join in with baby groups. I refused to take too much stock at this point – this was absolutely what I had and still did want and I could not afford to fall apart. I was afraid that if I began to cry I wouldn't be able to stop. It was the right decision for that time.

"Why am I so sad? There's a crack."

I cried all evening after I had spent the afternoon at the children's hospital with my son. I wasn't worried at all by this appointment for him to have an EEG. I was certain that he was and is fit and well and no one disagreed with me. I cried because I understood my own mother's experiences as a mother. I felt something simultaneously from both another person's experience and my own very early life. Pip and I had a lovely time at the hospital; an intense and enjoyable play. I had eyes and ears on everything, inventing games from our surroundings, preparing him for what was to come without leaving gaps for gruesome misinterpretation. Working out strategies to keep him still and calm while they glued things to his head to take readings of his brain activity levels. This was *my* childhood, playing 'scribble' on pads of paper in hospital corridors, examining every detail of murals in waiting rooms and creating stories, playing word games. I was my mother, thinking quickly, acting deftly, dispelling myths and asking questions to test understanding – always an eye on protecting the psyche.

You bring everything and all that you are to motherhood. You would love to just bring your 'best' parts to this most wonderful and important privilege, the bits you're happiest with under scrutiny. Your motherhood is wrapped up in your childhood just as and because your childhood was wrapped up in your mother's motherhood, which was also wrapped up in her childhood and so on in a cycle of myriad colours and flavours. To some extent, I repeated the motherhood I had witnessed.

Now, I am an imperfect mother. One who loves her little boy with all her might. One who relishes his wonderfulness, his capacity for joy, his fantastic imagination and cracking sense of humour. We have an amazing relationship. Some days I do an excellent job and sometimes I get it wrong. I am still healing. I keep reflecting and growing. On the many good days I am psychologically a well-healed person. On the fewer bad days I am a high functioning damaged person. Every day, I am going to do my best to reflect honestly on the day, learn from it, and continue to develop and deepen, hone and grow and to do it with love and with kindness; and also without guilt.

Chapter Thirteen – Shona

I approached the house, my steps slowing down the nearer I came. Looking up at the cold, dark structure that was my home, I took a deep breath and put my key in the lock. The door flew open to reveal my mum.

"What time do you call this? I told you to be home by ten."

I said nothing.

"Well? What have you got to say for yourself?"

What could I say? I'd narrowly missed the bus because I was waiting for my friend and didn't want to leave her to make her own way home late at night. All that could be heard was the ticking of the clock on the mantelpiece. When she was like this, red in the face, a pulse beating above her left eye, nothing was going to stop the inevitable.

I left home at the tender age of eighteen after yet another argument with my mum. On the day I left my mum uttered that immortal phrase: "If you go out that door, don't ever come back again." And she meant it. For the next four months she proceeded to ignore any attempt on my part to reconcile, pointedly walking past me as if I didn't exist whenever I came home to visit. Only the death of my thirteen-year-old brother four months later resulted in her talking to me again.

A year later on the anniversary of my brother's death, she took an overdose. She claimed that she only wanted to forget, but to me it looked as if my brother and sisters and I were not worth living for.

This was my experience of what it's like to be a mother.

At the age of twenty-five I was diagnosed with Sjögren's Syndrome, an autoimmune disease. I'd been ill quite a lot as a child, but my mum never believed me and said that I was a 'hypochondriac'. The doctor who broke the news made it sound as if I would be in a wheelchair by the time I was thirty. So when I started to feel broody we consulted the doctor. His response was that sometimes getting pregnant could help the condition to improve. What he didn't tell us was that it can also potentially harm the baby.

I fell pregnant very quickly and literally blossomed. I loved the whole experience and couldn't wait to be a mum. The nine months passed quickly and one Sunday in June I was admitted in the early stages of labour. After listening to the baby's heart, the midwife excused herself to go and find a doctor. Instinctively I knew that something was wrong. My baby's heart rate was half what it should be. At this point the doctors didn't know why and they prepared us for the worst. Three days later, I gave birth to a beautiful boy. It was love at first sight. His heart was damaged but was somehow managing to compensate and we were told that he was going to be alright. They also told me that it had been because of my illness that the damage had occurred.

I was devastated and for years carried around the guilt, thinking that it was my fault. Fortunately the heart is a marvellous organ and coped very well until my son was eleven years old, when he had to have a pacemaker inserted.

The first that my mum knew about all this was after he'd been born. It didn't even occur to me to ask for her support.

I didn't seem to be recovering from the birth. I gradually became unable to eat or drink. My GP sent me to see the consultant when my son was five weeks old. He put it down to post-natal depression and I accepted that; after all, according to my mum I was a 'hypochondriac'. But five weeks later I completely collapsed and by this time I couldn't even swallow a sip of water. For the next ten weeks I was subjected to humiliating tests as the doctors tried to find out what was wrong with me. My weight dropped dramatically and at one point I had a stroke and the doctors told my family that I might not make it. The doctors now decided that I had SLE, known as Lupus.

I was in a coma for three days and when I came round my mum was sitting by my bed. I took this as a sign that perhaps we could finally have a proper mother/daughter relationship, but things continued to be difficult. At this time the doctors advised me against having any more children. For three years I was more than happy with this. In fact the whole idea of risking going through this again terrified me. But I didn't factor in the strength of the maternal instinct.

When my son was four, my consultant unexpectedly told me they had come to the conclusion that my being ill had nothing to do with the pregnancy or birth. Apparently other similar cases he'd read about had been unrelated to pregnancy. He said that should I want to have more children they were confident that with close monitoring I would be alright. They also said there was a good chance that any future babies wouldn't be born with my son's heart condition and anyway, at this point he was living a normal life. My husband took a bit of persuading, but eventually I fell pregnant and settled in to await the new arrival.

During a routine check-up when I was twenty-three weeks pregnant the nurse had difficulty picking up a heartbeat, but put it down to the way the baby was facing. Two weeks later the same problem occurred so they decided to do a scan. This was the day after my son's fifth birthday. When the sonographer excused herself to go and fetch the doctor I knew that something was wrong. I was completely unprepared for what happened next: the baby was dead. I asked the doctor to call my in-laws as my husband was out of the country at the time. He was coming home later that day so it was arranged that I should be admitted the next day to be induced. At twenty-five weeks it's classed as a miscarriage, but you still have to give birth. I remember quietly enduring the pain of giving birth listening to another woman down the corridor screaming and resenting her because her baby was alive. How I got through it I'll never know. It was another little boy and three days after celebrating my eldest son's birthday, I said goodbye to his little brother.

Once again my own mother didn't even find out about what had happened until almost a week later. I couldn't face telling her. She hadn't been very happy when I'd told her that I was pregnant and I thought that she would say, "I told you so!" I sent my husband to tell her with instructions that I didn't want to see her, but to my surprise she insisted on coming. Once again I thought that at last my mum and I were going to be able to have some sort of relationship based on an equal footing, but things soon reverted to the normal situation of me being the one who had to call or visit and no matter how often I did, it was never enough. The loss of my son was never mentioned again, neither were there any enquiries about how I was coping.

A year later we moved to a completely different part of the country. The doctors at my old hospital had put the loss of my son down to being 'just one of those things' and didn't believe that it was anything to do with Lupus. We arranged to speak to a gynaecologist at my new hospital and he was very happy to support us if I wanted to try again. I never seemed to have any trouble getting pregnant and I soon called him with the news.

Growing up I'd observed that some of my friends seemed to have a close relationship with their mothers and actually enjoyed their company. I couldn't wait to leave mine. This had made me long for a daughter in the hope that I could experience this relationship for myself, at least as a mother. You can imagine how delighted I was when the twenty-one week scan revealed that it was a girl. Unfortunately we also found out that she was developing the same problem with her heart as my son. At first we weren't too concerned about it but two weeks later another scan showed that her heart was failing. I was immediately admitted and given drugs to bring the heart out of failure and prevent any more damage happening. After a couple of weeks the doctors were confident that she was going to be alright. The plan was to carry on with the drugs and to deliver her by Caesarean section at thirty-six weeks.

The drugs I was taking affected me quite badly but I was more than happy to put up with it if it meant that my baby was ok. At thirty-five weeks her heart rate suddenly plummeted and she was born by an emergency section and immediately operated on to insert a pacemaker. They transferred her to the Children's Intensive Care Unit, which was in a separate building. Despite having had major surgery, I made my way to be by her side every day. She would grasp my finger as I sang to her or told her stories. Every so often I would have to leave while the doctors did more tests or put in another tube. By this time the doctors had warned us that she could be severely disabled and I would lie awake making plans about how we were going to cope.

When she was fifteen days old the doctors told us they believed that due to a lack of oxygen around the time of her birth she would never be able to come off the ventilator and breathe on her own. They were going to carry out a special scan of her brain that would let them know for sure. Two days later the scan confirmed their suspicions. We'd been told that if what they suspected was true then it was only the machines that were keeping her alive. We were faced with one of the worst decisions any parent could ever be asked to make.

Later on that night I held her properly for the first time since she'd been born. Half an hour later I turned to the doctor and told them that she had gone. At first they didn't believe me as they'd warned us it could take hours. Knowing that she went quickly has helped me to come to terms with the decision we made. The machines would have kept her alive for a bit longer but the doctors said she would have been in pain. The day before, while sitting with her, I watched as she cried silent tears because of the tube in her throat and I knew then in my heart that she'd had enough.

My mum didn't come to the funeral. She didn't phone or write and when I did eventually see her five months later, we spent a week together doing 'nice' things and my daughter was never mentioned. I was in no place to bring it up.

I eventually had another son. The doctors told me of a way they thought they could prevent the baby's heart from becoming damaged. It was a risk. But I felt that although it would be hard if I lost another baby, it would be harder to live with the 'what if' of not at least trying.

Unsurprisingly I eventually ended up suffering from clinical depression. During this time my mum stopped speaking to me and although I went to see her when she was diagnosed with terminal cancer, we never really resolved anything. When she passed away, yes I was sad at the death of another human being, but in reality I felt that I had lost my mum years ago.

Why my mum was the way she was, I'll never know. I do remember that she had a massive chip on her shoulder. You never got a second chance with her and because of this she lost many friends. Even my dad eventually had enough and told her to leave when I was twenty. Mum was the eldest daughter in a family of thirteen. My gran, her mum, was a soft round gentle woman, very loving and caring, the complete opposite of my mum. My gran's house was always in chaos, housework being an alien concept to her. I know that my mum probably had a difficult upbringing. My granddad was work-shy and money was tight and being the eldest she probably had a lot of responsibility from an early age, being robbed of her childhood in the process. She did the same to me. I have memories of making breakfast for my brothers and sisters in a house we left when I was ten.

My mum didn't have much to do with her family when I was a child. When she married my dad she did work hard to better herself and I think she might have been ashamed of her roots. But oddly enough she was devastated when my gran died. But even on that occasion she shrugged me off when I tried to comfort her. My dad once asked me if I ever remembered my mum hugging me. I said no, I didn't. He replied, "That's because she never did." My sons were hugged to death.

Like everything else in life when it comes to parenting, we have a choice. We don't need to repeat the pattern of behaviour we grow up with. When asked I jokingly say that I learned my parenting skills from Home and Away and Neighbours. But it's not really very far from being the truth. I just knew that I wasn't going to treat my children the way I had been treated.

Perhaps it was my need to fill the gap where a mother's love should be that drove me on to go through so much to have my family. I only know that even when I was almost prostrate with grief, I was still there for my sons. My eldest son recently had to have an operation that resulted in complications. I was there every day alongside my daughter-in-law. After all, that's what mothers are meant to do – isn't it?

Chapter Fourteen – Sarah

Today, as I was walking my two children up to their primary school, my six-year-old daughter stopped me and said: *"You know, Mummy, you're such a good mummy."* Both children then gave me a huge hug. This was unexpected and certainly not in the usual course of events on the way to school!

Moments like this can easily reduce me to tears because my own childhood has created so many crises of confidence in my life, in my relationships, and most of all in my ability to be a parent.

When I was about four or five years old, my parents' relationship started to fall apart. During this period my mother and I started to live periodically with my grandparents. When my parents finally separated, my mother and I moved away for a couple of years before she met another man. This man did not want to bring up someone else's child. After a year or so of violence towards me, which my mother initially tried to hide, my grandmother witnessed it and gave my mother an ultimatum – her daughter or this man. My mother chose the man. It was decided at that point by the family that I would live with my aunt and uncle.

I remember the day that I moved to live with my aunt and uncle and my two older cousins. It was a beautiful day and I was feeling really quite excited. I think I thought it was going to be like another holiday as I had spent quite a bit of time at their house during summer holidays. As soon as we arrived at the house this time though, I was told straight away that I was now to call my aunt and uncle "Mum and Dad" and that my cousins would be my "brothers". My mother was now my "aunt" and I was never to discuss anything that had happened before that day with anyone either in the family or outside it. My name was changed to their name. The few little bits and bobs from my old life that I had brought with me that my mother had packed for me were taken away from me and I never saw them again. My oldest cousin, who at this time was nineteen years old, even pushed me into a room that day and told me that I would never really be a member of this family so not to get used to being there.

This was a bewildering turn of events. My world had turned upside down and I retreated further into myself, feeling that everything about me was something to be ashamed of, and that I was unwanted by my own parents and unwelcome in my new home.

My aunt and uncle were very controlling, but were not unkind. At Christmas and birthdays I was showered with gifts, but they never demonstrated any kind of love towards me. I have no memories of getting cuddled by them or even them chatting to me in an interested way. I was often made to feel that any opinions I had were not valid and that I was a background distraction. I felt that everything was my fault and if I'd done things differently everyone would have been much happier. I also continually thought I was dreaming and that I would wake up one morning back with my own mother and father living a normal life.

Despite my crushing shyness, I made friends in my new school but I often felt lonely and was most comfortable cuddled up with the dog and a book. I spoke to my mother on the phone once a year on my birthday.

As I grew older, I became more interested in my own parents. My father was an absolute no-go area. I attended the christenings of my mother's two new children and this seemed to stir up a lot of emotions for me and I became a bit unruly for a while. My uncle had begun drinking heavily and for years we could barely be in the same room as each other. I became obsessed with my father but no one would tell me anything about him. My aunt and uncle would say repeatedly that I was just like him. This was not intended as a compliment but I was happy to be associated with him because I felt so disconnected where I was. Frustration and guilt built up and I think it was probably around the age of fourteen that I had my first severe bout of depression. A doctor suggested to my aunt that I have some counselling but my aunt said it was ridiculous. It was also around this time that I realised that I had some kind of inner determination that things would improve, if only I worked hard. Luckily I was a bright child. I put my head down and worked to make sure I got into university at eighteen.

I enjoyed university and the freedom I had away from home but just before I sat my finals my grandparents died a couple of weeks apart. Their deaths affected me enormously and within a few months my depression returned with a vengeance. I managed to secure the perfect job but I stopped eating and developed anorexia nervosa. I also drank heavily in a way I can only describe as a form of alcohol bulimia. I drank and made myself throw up so I wouldn't have a hangover and could go into work the next day. I began to self-harm and put myself into dangerous situations. This went on for some time. Thankfully, after one hospitalisation, it was suggested that I see a different type of therapist. My life changed at our first meeting. I hadn't been able to speak about my childhood to anyone during those terrible years. She allowed me to sit in silence for as long as I needed, and after a few sessions I began to open up.

After a few years of therapy, I met a man who I started a relationship with and after a while he suggested we live together. I had never entertained the idea of settling down and certainly never thought I'd have any children. I had discovered that not only had my mother given her child away, but my grandmother had also given away two of her own children. It seemed to me like a family curse and if I didn't have any children I'd break the curse. Then I got pregnant.

I knew I was pregnant immediately. Even before doing the pregnancy test, I could do nothing but be sick. I had a severe form of hyperemesis gravidarum. I was sick non-stop. All I could do was lie in bed; even turning over would make me sick. After a couple of weeks I was hospitalised and fed with a drip. I was let out after a week but only managed to get to the supermarket car park on the way home before it started again. I was hospitalised again the next day. The nurses often told me not to worry because my baby was perfectly healthy. I didn't really care whether my baby was healthy or not because I felt so awful. I had a friend who was pregnant with her first child at the same time as me who was still running half marathons. I could barely get out of bed!

I had read that hyperemesis could be a psychological problem and I started to worry that I was only being sick because I didn't want the baby. Thinking those things didn't stop the sickness; it continued throughout. I had a dreadful delivery, three weeks early. I had hours of back-to-back labour without any pain relief (I had gone into myself and hadn't been able to ask for anything). When she delivered I haemorrhaged and there was no O-negative blood available in the hospital. I had to have iron tablets and was absolutely exhausted. The nurses only brought my daughter over the first few days of her life when she needed feeding, then took her away to the nursery. It wasn't until we got her home that I actually spent any time with her. I had a huge crisis of confidence. I had no idea what I was doing and she just screamed all the time. This was a time in my life when I wished I had a mother to help me because I felt completely out of my depth.

My daughter was a challenging baby and the midwives and the health visitors tried to help me get her to feed and sleep properly. Nothing worked. For that first year, it was crazy. We had virtually no sleep and I suffered from post-natal depression. I felt useless as a mother and the continual whisper in my head was that I was just like my own mother and grandmother and not cut out for motherhood. As my daughter's weight dropped and her tantrums began to escalate the health visitors kept telling me I wasn't doing anything wrong but I knew I was struggling. My own health began to deteriorate. I had eaten so little while pregnant that when I tried to reintroduce food I began to have food intolerances. It turned out to be coeliac, which I had no control over, but before it was diagnosed I blamed myself for not making myself eat properly while pregnant. I had my gall bladder removed but waited until the last possible moment because I was breastfeeding and was too scared to leave my daughter. This delay resulted in my closest to death experience to date. Even the doctor said he didn't think I was going to make it. I had written a letter to my daughter before I went in for surgery because I didn't think I'd see her again, and I wanted her to know that I loved her.

Not two months after the gall bladder surgery, I was pregnant again. Again, I knew straight away. This time after

I saw the positive pregnancy test I lay on the bathroom floor and cried. I couldn't bear to go through it all again but I also knew I couldn't get rid of the baby. The doctor straight away gave me anti-sickness injections, suppositories and tablets to keep on top of the hyperemesis. As a result the start of the pregnancy was easier. This time though I developed gestational diabetes, which resulted in a very big baby. I was dilating from 29 weeks, and from about 35 weeks I couldn't walk and was kept in the hospital. A couple of weeks later he was born, all 10lbs of him. And I'm a very small woman...

From the moment he was born, there was something different about me. Whether I had more confidence or he was just a more settled baby, I'm not sure. I didn't have to try to get him to feed; he just knew what to do. When the nurses took him through to the maternity nursery, I went through, brought him back and took him into bed with me. Later when we went home, he fed and slept easily. He went to bed in his crib and when he woke during the night I brought him into bed with me where he'd sleep until the morning.

When my son became seriously ill at eight months old, I first went into denial then, over the course of a couple of days, I flipped into a woman crazy with fear of losing her child. I had a stand-up argument with God pleading with him to take me rather than my son. My aunt and uncle had been fiercely religious, something I had long abandoned, but it came flooding back at a time of extreme need. My son pulled through but I now have a niggling worry at the back of my mind that I might, at some point, have to pay the price. I think that's one of the consequences of my interrupted childhood – because I took the blame for everything at such a young age, I can have an over-inflated sense of myself, that I could keep my son alive by doing a deal with God.

Over the last few years, I have read every parenting book available to me. I have worried over every parenting decision I have made, often blaming my own childhood on things I have felt out of my control. Growing up without my parents has always made me feel as if I have been drifting around without any ties to keep me secure, steady and grounded. My interrupted childhood will forever have made me into a different person to the one I left behind the day I moved to live with my aunt and uncle. Relationships of all sorts are difficult for me. I still find it easier to cuddle up with one of my pets than with my partner. I have recently realised that my two children don't have that difficulty and they would cuddle me from morning until night given the opportunity. They have managed to ground me in a way my own family never did.

I am fiercely independent. Throughout everything I have continued to work and now run a successful business while looking after my children. It is vitally important for me to know that I would be financially able to look after myself and my children if anything happened to my partner. My biggest anxieties in life today are that something will happen to me and my children will grow up without a mother, or that something happens to them and I'll be left without them. I know these are probably every mother's greatest fears but they are a palpable anxiety every day for me. A school trip to the pantomime when my daughter has to go on a bus without me, or when my son is driven to a party by someone other than me can make me feel physically sick. However, I allow them to go on these trips because I know that stopping them from doing these things will probably alienate them from me in the long run. And hopefully the more they do these things, the easier it will be for me.

My daughter is now at the age I was when my childhood had started to unravel and this sometimes causes conflicting emotions in me. Sometimes when I look at her I see the little girl I once was and feel sad for my younger self, and other times when she's in the middle of a full-scale tantrum because I won't buy her an iPad I get angry because they have so many things and, most importantly, they have as much love as I can possibly give, which I didn't receive from my parents. However, probably the most important thing I've learned since becoming a mother is not to project my childhood onto my children, particularly my daughter. They are growing up to be two wonderful children and in part, that is because my daughter was right this morning when she said I was "a good mummy". I try my hardest and I'm learning more every day.

Chapter Fifteen – Joanna

When I was a little girl, I didn't think about getting married or having babies – I had a few dolls but I treated them like friends, rather than pretending to be a mother. My relationship with my mother was not great when I was growing up, which is maybe why I didn't play "mummy". She was a primary school teacher who referred to the children she taught as "her kids". I was extremely jealous because the mother that I came home to was always marking "her kids'" papers and planning for lessons and activities that I was not going to be a part of since I wasn't in her class, nor did I even go to the same school. We were not close and I felt like an outsider for most of my childhood and teenage years.

When I was 17, my grandmother died. My mother went to be with her and through my other grandmother's gossip I discovered that whilst on her deathbed, my grandmother had batted away my mother's attempts to hold her hand. I realised that my relationship with my mother was a mirror of the relationship she had with her mother and if I wanted it to change, I would have to do the changing. So I started saying "I love you" to my mother every day. At first she didn't say it back; she just looked at me quizzically and said, "That's nice, dear." Eventually, she started to say it too. In those days I saw my mother as a mother and not as a person. In fact, I used to look at her and think "Who is this woman?"

I eventually moved away to Seattle and didn't see much of my parents for about five years. I have always been into personal development and it was during one seminar that I realised I was the one pushing and keeping my mother at a distance. I remember a particularly painful memory of my brother and me sitting having dinner with my parents and playing a game we used to play called General Knowledge. The rest of my family was really good at retaining useless information but I had no interest and was therefore not very good at it. They kept stock questions they knew I knew the answer to and would throw a few out at me if I was starting to get upset that I didn't know any of the answers to the current questions. I should point out I was about 12 years old at the time.

My mother asked me a question I didn't know the answer to and she guffawed, and I stormed away shouting "I guess I'm stupid." And that is the moment that dictated how I reacted to my mother. I was always trying to prove to her that I wasn't stupid, or I would snap at her out of the blue if I felt inferior. This continued until that seminar when I was 27. At the seminar, I recalled details of our various interactions throughout the years and in all cases, I was the one who said or felt I was inadequate. Never had my mother ever actually said those words to me. I called her during the seminar to apologise for my behaviour, explaining that the reason I acted the way I had was because I thought she thought I was stupid. Well, to hear my mother say "I would never call you stupid, it's simply not true" was a pivotal point in my life and my relationship with my mother changed in an instant. I started to get to know her as a person. I'm now 42 and I can honestly say she is my best friend and knows me best.

I came to motherhood later than usual as I had previously been in a marriage where children were not in the equation. I had spent some time with friends who had two daughters and it was then that I realised I felt a void. Imagine my surprise when I woke up, almost 36 years old, with the sudden realisation that I wanted to be a mother.

I am grateful that I didn't leave it too late and that I have a very spirited and healthy baby boy. Having an established business and being older and therefore somewhat more set in my ways, I suppose I had rose-coloured spectacles tainting my vision of motherhood. I was excited by the new role and the new responsibilities – I suppose I approached it like a job description! So where I felt secondary to my own mother's career, I put motherhood front and centre. I didn't want work to come between me and raising my son. And when I had trouble breastfeeding, I put everything into making it work.

I was amazed that I had the determination and commitment to overcome the challenge of breastfeeding. I realised that where I thought I lacked a certain drive to achieve, I had never actually chosen to undertake anything that I was so passionate about and committed to seeing it work. However, after nine months of staying at home, I realised that I had lost my sense of identity and if truth be told, my son was getting a bit bored. My son is very sociable so I thought going to nursery would suit him, and enable me to work a little. I needed to be out in the world a bit more and I also found myself craving people to talk to – I realised that I needed to find someone to talk to who would just listen.

So I found a therapist to work with me on integrating my role as a mother with my other roles. I found my challenge was that when I decided to become a mother, I basically decided to put my own life on hold. It might sound cliché to say that being a mother is the best thing I ever did and it's hard to imagine my life before Christopher. But I realised through my work with my therapist that I have spent most of my life avoiding immersing myself in a career for fear of turning into a workaholic like my mother. I used to be career driven and when I realised that I was becoming too absorbed in my career at the expense of my personal life, I left that line of work and completely shut out those skills and habits. I then became self-employed and in retrospect, I see that I tended to restrict the amount of hours and type of work I did.

What is fascinating is that it transpires that I have been inadvertently rushing my son to grow up so I could "get my life back"! Because my own mother was a workaholic, I didn't have a role model to show me that you can be a mother AND have a career. So when he was an infant, I was looking forward to the day he could sit up on his own. When he could do that, I was looking forward to his crawling. Now, I can't wait for him to walk – etc...!! The internal work that I am now doing is helping me to integrate both having a life and being a mother so I can thrive in my work and enjoy my son every step of his journey without rushing him to grow up!

Blending multiple aspects of living into a harmonious whole is something I realise I am passionate about and I will see it work; the overcoming of my breastfeeding challenge has shown me what I am capable of achieving when I am committed. In some ways, motherhood has given me my life back as I am learning to trust my passion for my work and my role of being a mother without fear of becoming lost in either.

Chapter Sixteen – Kate

This is the story of my mother and me; how our relationship changed and the influence she had on my efforts at mothering my own children.

First, basic facts: I was born in WW2; my father was a pilot in the RAF and was killed when I was nine months old. My mother went back to live and work in London, while I was brought up by loving grandparents. I was cherished, and aware of it. There is nothing to be sorry about here. I knew no other way and there were many others in the same boat. Most of my early friends were adopted only children. If a family adopted a child, and there were plenty available, the wife was spared war work; not the best motivation, you might think. But we were all happy children being well cared for by wartime standards, with my only regret looking back being that I never knew my father. Memories of air raids and doodlebugs are in there somewhere, but rationing and austerity had no effect on me. What you don't know, you don't miss.

I was vaguely aware of my mother coming and going, but I don't remember her as a mother figure; she cared greatly about appearance and spent hours making me clothes from unravelled sweaters, parachute silk, or an elderly aunt's old nightdress. Little smocked dresses, or a flannel suit with perfect lining, dungarees knitted from Shetland wool: these are vivid memories which even now, more than sixty years later, I can smell and feel. I was her doll and it is no coincidence that she also hand-made exquisite clothes for my own doll. So she cared for me, but like most very young children I was not particularly aware of the depth of her feeling. I am sure it was there, but it must have been hard for a widow of 22, and an attractive one at that, to have a life knowing that whatever decisions she made her young daughter was paramount. Meanwhile Grannie was sweet, kind and caring. I was fortunate.

In much later life Mum told me more about this time. She spoke of being told my father was dead, picking herself up pretty quickly and getting back to work. She had numerous boyfriends: dashing young men, glamorous, adventurous and desirable; a pretty typical wartime scenario. When I was seven she married my stepfather, a worthy, solid, much older man, at which stage I moved in with them and a completely new phase of life started. He adored my mum and me in the truest way, and being a successful accountant in corporate practice was more than able to provide for us. Later, Mum told me this was the reason she married him, for what he gave me. But he was dull and although their marriage survived I was aware of her difficulties and, it seemed, inevitable attraction to other men.

I was sent away to boarding school, yet at no stage did I feel rejected or unloved at being sent away from home. I was told it would be good for me; other friends were experiencing the same. In retrospect, I don't think it did me anything but good.

It was a single-sex life. So boys were alien, glamorous and desirable, because I didn't have any experience of them in a day to day situation. Having left school and compliantly done what I was asked – to undergo a deadly, rigorous secretarial course – I still lived at home. There were some very nice young men I went out with who came to see me, often arriving before I got home. Much later I heard from them, or from my mother, that when collecting me from home they would arrive early to see her, that they fancied her and heaven knows what else. Fortunately, and naively, I was unaware at the time. However, many years later when my then husband and she had sex in the bedroom next to ours, while I lay frozen and paralysed, I started to think more deeply about her attitude to the men in my life. And when he told me that sexually she was "just like me", I was traumatised beyond belief. Even recalling that phrase makes me feel sick.

Prior to this I adored her. I couldn't imagine life without her. She was immensely supportive when we were young, struggling parents. She dressed up my boys in clothes we could not afford; can you spot a thread here? She gave us food parcels and took charge of the boys. Because she was easily young enough to be their mother, when she took them out she loved being taken for their mum. She looked after them wonderfully well, to the point that today they both have loving memories of her.

But that ultimate betrayal changed everything for me. My conclusion is she was jealous of me. Also, both she and my husband 'enjoyed' drink. It was the middle of the end of my marriage. And was certainly the end of my loving relationship with Mum. However, we stayed very much in touch and on the surface nothing changed. In fact, I am pretty sure she forgot all about that time. Sadly, I've not found that possible although I have managed forgiveness.

She came to need my support more than I needed hers: that subtle shift from cared for to carer. In her last years she was a rip-roaring alcoholic who had a seizure when she could no longer get to the bottle, after which I helped her dry out rather than letting her be admitted to hospital. I'd had plenty of experience of the process with my husband. This entailed three weeks sleeping on her sitting room floor, administering medication and loads of positive encouragement. It also meant enduring heavy cigarette smoke lying low in the room, but she needed a crutch. There were lavatorial accidents, big ones, requiring washing her exactly as we do babies. The image of her lying whimpering on her bed, naked, covered in faeces, will stay with me for life. I promise I was gentle cleaning her up and putting her back into a clean bed; desperate, revolted but gentle. This is nothing more than carers and nurses have to do, but there is something ultra-poignant about doing for your mother what she did for you as a baby.

So what sort of mother was I? I cannot judge, but I do know my frailties were human and often the product of wanting everyone to be happy.

I was pregnant before marriage, and very young. There was no question of having to get married as the family said they would support me whatever my decision. However, I was convinced that marriage was the answer. The shame my parents felt must have been extreme, as they arranged for us to get married as far away from home as was decent. After all, this was the early 60s when in bourgeois society only very strong characters could get away with feeling no guilt. As a young mother it all came naturally to me and I loved both my boys as much as every mum should. My concern now is that I should have been much stronger and stricter when things started to go wrong for one of them. I should have been more protective, given more guidance and support. I was terrified of conflict with my children, a relic of my childhood and my phobia of argument and conflict. But boy, did I love them. And now we are all three very close. They still need my support and I theirs.

My mother is remembered as a super granny by my children and as a damaged personality by me. They will never know how it really was.

Chapter Seventeen – Isobel

A little girl, three years old, with two blonde pigtails and a hand-me-down blue woollen coat, arrives at her nursery - a large residential house with an imposing doorway. It's located down a long lane on the outskirts of a northern town. She gets out of the car; her father drives off to work. She wishes he had taken her in. She is too short to reach the doorbell and her quiet knocking (don't want to make a fuss) doesn't bring anyone so she wanders round to the back of the house. Through the windows she sees a group of children playing. She waves at them nervously to attract their attention so they will open the door quickly before she gets in trouble. They smile, wave back and return to their game. She feels sad and rejected. Why don't they want to play with her?

She doesn't bang on the window (that's drawing too much attention); she doesn't wait at the main door for new arrivals. If they don't want me, she thinks, I'll go somewhere else.

She trots down the muddy lane, and turns left onto the main road into town, busy with its early morning traffic. It begins to rain. The big lorries splatter her coat as they thunder past. She follows the road for a mile until she gets to a pedestrian crossing.

She waits patiently for the lights to change.

A woman, standing next to her, grabs her hand.

"Would you like some help crossing the road?" she says. She has no choice but to walk across with the stranger. She smiles nervously on the other side and manages to take her hand out of the woman's grip. She turns left, and hurries on her way. A car slows down. She sees the driver staring at her. She crosses a few smaller roads and makes a right up the hill, tracing the way she's subconsciously memorised, to her father's factory. She feels safer now. But when she arrives at the imposing building, with its impenetrable facade and wire mesh fence, she becomes nervous and anxious – she realises that she doesn't know where his office is. She opens the door, finds someone to ask, and is taken upstairs. Upon seeing her, a small, unexpected figure in the doorway, her father lets out "Bloody hellfire!" in his thick Yorkshire accent.

That little girl was me, and this is one of my first memories. It is still as vivid forty odd years later as when it happened. I've always been quite proud of that little girl making such a long and potentially dangerous journey. At her determination, spatial awareness, self-sufficiency, memory, bravery, confidence and independence. But recently I've looked at the incident through a different lens. Through the eyes of a nurturing mother to a beautiful blonde haired girl and boy. Through the eyes of having discovered something about my upbringing. And I've wondered why on earth did I do that? Why did I think undertaking such a hazardous journey was more logical than banging louder on the door and making a noise? Why did I make such damning conclusions about myself?

The jigsaw puzzle is starting to make sense now. But back then, I was just a child trying to find a place in the world.

At each stage of the journey I made as that little girl walking in an adult's world, I can remember what I felt. And those feelings were created by a thought. I had internalised a belief system that was formed by my upbringing. By the grand old age of three, this is what I'd learnt: that I was not wanted, was unloved and unlovable. Always an outsider. That I didn't ask for, or need, help because I wasn't worth it. I was misunderstood and rejected. Abandoned by those who should have been protecting me the most.

What the hell happened for me to think all that, aged three?

*

We were the quintessentially middle class family – large house in the country, father who owned his own business, three bright and able children with manners. Except we were hiding a secret. A secret we didn't realise we were hiding, something that didn't have a name. An insidious form of mental, emotional and physical abuse which we sort of knew was not normal but couldn't do anything about.

My mother, though we didn't know it then, has Narcissistic Personality Disorder.

*

The best quote I've read about the condition is: "People with NPD don't suffer from it. The people around them suffer from it." In their mind, there's nothing wrong with them – it's everyone else who's the problem. They can feel no empathy. Their children exist only as an extension of themselves, not as individuals who need parental (emotional, spiritual, or age appropriate) guidance to grow into fully formed, emotionally healthy adults. Interest in their lives exists only in so far as it reflects well on them; we exist to make them look good.

The irony of this condition is that diagnosis is difficult as the narcissist is so self-absorbed that he or she is unlikely to seek professional help. They view themselves as perfect and far superior to anyone else. Therapy is therefore not an option. It is often the therapist of the child who diagnoses the parent. In our case, as we grew older, we recognised that how we were treated was pathological. Working out there was something clinically wrong primarily came about through my sister's pain of losing a child and our mother's truly wicked comments; things that no grieving mother should ever have to hear, especially not from her own mother.

It's been a very private, painful journey to this point. Well-meaning friends say that their mothers were also 'difficult' or embarrassing or sometimes said terrible things to them. But did their mothers celebrate their daughter's birthday for the first seven years of life on the wrong date, only corrected when my brother found my birth certificate in the safe? Or try to convince you that your own son was born in June when in fact he was born in March? I laugh about it all now – humour is a great antidote to the emotional sting of not being cared about, but back then we led a double life.

To the outside world, she was seen as well-meaning but 'eccentric'; behind closed doors we had to deal with pathological lying, unfounded accusations, emotional instability, vicious verbal attacks, the complete inability to accept reality, emotional blackmail and bullying, deprivation, emotional and physical neglect, social isolation, pitting one sibling against another, blame shifting, our dreams and desires either not acknowledged or squashed – all whilst having to accept her fantasist notions in her own expertise / beauty / intelligence / superiority without any support or understanding of our own needs as children.

I was constantly being sabotaged, whether that was by creating a massive argument before my driving test (which only made me more determined to pass so I could have a modicum of freedom), making me one hour late for a three hour O level exam or disrupting my graduation ceremony so that she became the centre of attention. She would sabotage my efforts because she didn't achieve the dizzying heights of success that she thought she deserved. She didn't want her daughter to outshine her.

On the occasions I did do something laudable, she would take all the credit. On a day to day basis, it was more manipulative and insidious. She would twist logic so that my developing sense of the world and my place in it was questioned; or she undermined me, subtly phrasing things in certain ways so that it came out as supportive, parental advice. Some phrases were more blatant –

You were a mistake

You have ruined my life

You're imagining things

You're overreacting/too oversensitive

You're just immature

You don't know what you're talking about

What is wrong with you?

I've sacrificed everything for you

You are such a burden

I've come to realise that growing up was mainly about survival. I have few happy childhood memories. I have used amnesia as a form of coping strategy – if you can't remember, you can't be hurt, right? Except by burying things deeper they're harder to locate. But now I'm unpeeling the layers, I think of some of the stories my siblings remember as so preposterous that they would be funny if they weren't so poignant. Like the time when we went on holiday to Wales and the rest of the family went out on a boat for a few hours, leaving me in a Moses basket on the beach, only to return as the tide was coming in fast. My brother remembers panicking that they weren't going to reach me in time.

And then I think: Where on earth was Dad in all of this? The term for his role is enabler – he had been so beaten down that he had no inner resources to stand up for himself, let alone us. Consequently he was battling his own demons and frustrated potential, and was viciously, verbally abused, which resulted in untreated depression and an early death. He did the best he could. There are many great values that I learnt from him to counter the influence of my mother.

By the time I turned 18, I thought I was very good at not taking any of her cruel behaviours to heart. Which was just as well because I received a cracking present from her that year – an ill-conceived and poorly executed painting she had bought at auction for £5 that depicted the Devil.

Of course I was still desperate for maternal love but just didn't have the awareness or language to verbalise it. When my father died a few years later (we weren't allowed to grieve for a lost father; it was all about how she had lost her marvellous husband and how she had loved him so much), I thought I was searching for a replacement to teach me about the world, a father figure; in reality all I had ever wanted was to see what maternal love felt like. To have unconditional support and not feel the desperate loneliness, isolation and emptiness of being 'unmothered', which I had papered over with a cheery personality. I was, even at 21, eager to please her, and craved support and encouragement. However, I knew instinctively that her behaviour was abhorrent and that distance was the only way to protect myself – it was such a relief to move to London for university because I knew I would never, ever, ever, ever have to live under her roof and control again.

After my degree, I moved to the States. And after that, travelled around Asia and Australia. Even that created competition. Of course she trumped me by returning to England from her travels, aged 60 something, with a Gambian husband aged 24, in addition to being the sole benefactor to a whole village and its dog. And the way we found out? By seeing a 'Congratulations on your Wedding' card sent by the local WI.

Narcissists don't change. It is the people around them that must adjust their perspectives. So I have minimised contact with her. Some people find that difficult to comprehend. Cutting Mum out of my life? Well, she was never in it! I certainly don't want my children to be influenced by her, not now I'm experiencing the wonderful intensity of maternal love on the other side. I've done the grieving for the child I never got to be; for the expectation and hope that we could ever have a meaningful and loving relationship. I shall forever be disappointed if I'm looking for a maternal love that I never had – so I've stopped looking. The pain and sense of loss has disappeared. I have learnt to forgive and accept and move on.

I had a dream quite a while back that I was posting an obituary on Facebook, of all places. It started off something like this:

"This morning I had a phone call to tell me my mother had died. Hooray. What a relief. Now I can really call myself an orphan without pretending. I never had a mother. The woman who was my mother in name only is now physically gone."

That sounds so bitter and twisted and malevolent and angry. Yes, I have been all those things but I don't wish to be any of them now. Now I know she has NPD, now that the pieces have slotted together; now that I have accepted that she can't help herself, that we never had and never will have a healthy mother/daughter relationship, I have stopped craving maternal love. It's actually a relief to know that she has NPD. I'm not condoning her behaviour, but I know she can't change and that to manage the relationship from here, it is me who needs to manage my past and expectations.

It's a terrible thing to wish someone dead. But I can forgive myself for having once thought that. Feelings have a context. Thoughts have a context. I can now choose to either hold on to my story or move on. It's OK now because I can accept that that was just the way it was. Why should I base beliefs about myself on such an unreliable source?

My internal voice has been in overdrive, interpreting events of my childhood and shaping my adulthood, and I'm learning now to be aware of that voice and what the slant of the story is. It doesn't have to be a negative outcome. I can't rewrite history, nor change my past, but I can re-define how I interpret it, and make different conclusions. I can draw on the positives and build on the strengths that are part of me.

By questioning how I came to have such a negative inner voice, I've changed the way I feel about that formative event. My story has been rewritten:

I'm three years old, with a big smile, two blonde pigtails and a blue woollen coat with a fake fur collar, arriving at my nursery – a large residential house with an imposing doorway. It's located down a long lane on the outskirts of a northern town. I get out of the car; my father drives off to work. I am too short to reach the doorbell and my quiet knocking doesn't bring anyone so instead of being defeated, I think of how else I can get into the building. I wander round to the back of the house. Through the windows I see a group of children playing. I'd love to join them. I wave at them to attract their attention so they will open the door. They smile, wave back and return to their game.

That didn't work out how I wanted. Never mind. I've got a better plan! I'm off on an adventure.

I trot down the muddy lane, and turn left onto the main road into town, busy with its early morning traffic. I know exactly where I'm going. It starts to rain. As the big lorries thunder past, I follow the road for a mile until I get to a pedestrian crossing.

I wait patiently for the lights to change.

"Would you like some help crossing the road?" asks a woman standing next to me. I see the look of horror on her face but she really doesn't need to worry because this is the easy bit and I know what I'm doing.

I take her hand, more for her satisfaction than my need, and cross the road with the stranger. On the other side, I let go of the woman's warm grip, and turn left. I cross a few smaller roads and turn right up the hill, tracing the way I've subconsciously memorised, to my father's factory. Only when I arrive at the imposing building, with its impenetrable facade and wire mesh fence, do I become a little anxious - I realise that I don't know where his office is! Never mind, I'm sure I'll work something out. I feel safe. And proud that I have navigated the busy roads all on my own. I open the door, find someone to ask, and am taken upstairs. Upon seeing me, a self-sufficient and determined young girl in the doorway, my father lets out "Bloody hellfire!" in his thick Yorkshire accent.

Chapter Eighteen – Sarah P

From the age of five I was brought up by a single mother. It was the early '70s, divorce was still relatively unusual and I didn't know anyone else whose relationship with their father was restricted to a fortnightly weekend. That said, I leveraged this fact any which way – especially in the case of homework which, left undone by me, was excused as being left at my dad's.

I maintained I was not touched by this divorce; I vigorously extolled the virtues of two of everything. Except that wasn't really the case – with the exception of having two parents, even if only one was accessible on a daily basis. I kept this spin on my childhood right into my thirties and I truly honestly believed it.

In those days you didn't tell kids anything very much; situations were presented fait accompli and questions were not encouraged. I've revisited the explanations to ensure I really wasn't made to understand, and my memories of this time are patchy to say the least.

It was only many years later that the lack of memories began to bother me, but that is another story for another time, though intricately linked to this one of course. I am the thread that binds as will the next generation also be.

I always respected my mother for her achievements and, in an unspoken fashion, appreciated the challenges she overcame.

I didn't think twice about how I came to be the adventurous, gregarious, confident adult, brimful of optimism, that I was through my twenties and thirties. Does anyone? Should anyone? I don't think so – it's the way it should be, and I hope my own daughter springboards off me in an even more spectacular way.

I really lived the life in those years. I was young and self-obsessed. I was probably quite reckless and I flitted from bar job to motorcycle courier without any long term plan. I never ever thought there wasn't something I couldn't do – I had supreme self-confidence and my mother never ever questioned what was to become of me. Perhaps she did, but out of my earshot.

Through today's lens I marvel now at how disconnected our relationship was during my late teens and twenties. I wonder if it's normal, if it's a natural continuation of the separation that begins in the angst of the teenage years or if this distance was always a facet of our relationship.

If I allow myself to consider the future I am chilled at the thought of being equally disconnected from the daughter I adore with every fibre of my being. My chills are compounded with the realisation that this could well coincide with the loss of my own mother – although I fully expect her to make a hundred, as her mother did before; we are a long lived, strong willed female line.

There are many things about my mother that have frustrated me, exasperated me and sometimes infuriated me over the years but now as I skid down the over forty five hill towards fifty and she has eighty in her sights we are the closest we have ever been – at least given my patchy memory of childhood.

In my gratitude circle this fact appears often because it is not simply a product of the mellowing of the child and the ageing of the parent. It is the hard won affection and respect born out of shared diversity.

It is a very small sliver of a silver lining to compensate for nearly a decade of turbulence and turmoil.

Eight years ago I became a mother myself. I went into labour at 1:30am on a Wednesday morning and I was just about four weeks ahead of my due date. The last six weeks of my pregnancy hadn't been easy as I had to inject myself daily with insulin, and my husband was sliding deeper into a depression I didn't know he had.

I had kept my mother at arm's length during this time; I couldn't pretend all was well and so I kept my distance. When my now ex-husband rang her at around 1pm-ish to tell her my daughter had arrived by emergency c-section after twelve hours of labour her words were "My baby has had a baby." I think she told the woman on the till at the counter in M&S as that's where she was at the time!

My mother was thrilled about her third grandchild, unexpected at my grand old age of 39 and having only been married a few months.

I was just as thrilled to be a mother, but the shock of a new-born nearly a month early (no complications thankfully) was more than anything I could have anticipated. Within a month my husband had succumbed to his depression and one Wednesday evening we had the most dreadful row.

On the following Friday he saw a counsellor, I think for his second session, and either that evening or during the next day he went for a run and didn't return. A text some time later told me he had left. Whilst I had been tending to my daughter he had been throwing his things out of the bedroom window into the garden below. When he left to "go running" a cab was waiting beyond the garden fence.

I spent the night sitting on the sofa holding my daughter. I think I may have dozed but that was all.

In the morning I called my mum and she came immediately. I expected an onslaught of questions and an outpouring of opinions and judgments. There were a few of each, but nothing like the amount I was expecting.

And so for six weeks I had no idea where he was. Contact was sporadic and by text, and I knew he was within a fifty mile radius. That was all.

My mum came and stayed quite frequently, but not excessively. She did the practical stuff – cooked and cleaned – and sometimes I got frustrated because I wanted her to take the baby so I could do the washing up just for a change!

As time passed she stayed less frequently. My husband resurfaced and a few months later we sold the house and I moved into a small cottage. He stayed at his parents' some 10 miles away and we saw him maybe once a week.

The first three years of my daughter's life were a higgledy piggledy mess of trying to save the marriage amidst house moves and relocations. Working, mothering, moving and just enduring the upheavals. Adoring my daughter but not really 100% present in anything. It is only now, looking back, that I wonder what those early years might have been. I do not subscribe to regret or question what I might have done or missed out on, however. I did the best I could and my daughter thrived – even though I did not.

I had already decided divorce was the only option. I had to step out of the uncertainty of a barely present husband on whom I could not even rely to answer the phone.

Shortly after my daughter's third birthday my life took a completely unexpected turn when my elder brother, a single father himself, fell down some stairs. He sustained a horrendous head injury from which he barely survived, resulting in catastrophic brain damage.

Six months later, as he lay in a virtually catatonic state, I was catapulted from single mother of one toddler to parenting my 17 year old nephew and 15 year old niece.

We all moved into a new house in a new suburb together and began the journey of the last half decade.

It has been, without a doubt, the single most challenging period of my life. I never ever imagined I would be a single parent – hence why I came to motherhood late. To accelerate from toddler to teen overnight, and troubled teen at that, whilst dealing with the fallout from my brother's accident and subsequent recovery, required reserves of strength and resilience I was frankly pretty short on.

The working, mothering, enduring pattern continued. Only now there were the complexities of a disengaged, very angry young man to contend with, as well as a young girl maturing and facing the first real tests and big questions about her future in her GCSEs etc.

As these two young adults approached the end of their school lives, my own daughter began hers. One day I was at nursery discussing the phonics system, the next I was with a 6th form head of year discussing absence and attitude, and then at a Year 10 parents' evening discussing homework and university options.

Intermingled with this were misdemeanours that brought the police to our door, angst over boyfriends and arguments with girlfriends. Surgery after surgery for my brother, their father, who was wheelchair bound, doubly incontinent and non-verbal.

My mother and step-father, taking roles that were never planned for. Running my brother's business, assuming power of attorney and handling finances alongside parenting and grandparenting. Worried sick for their children and grandchildren.

The accident robbed us of our traditional roles. As a family we redefined them without a set of instructions. We wrought our new relationships from the fire and ice of our circumstances and they have been hard won.

They are still hot to touch, sometimes molten, and will forever be malleable in the heat of the aftermath. Despite our exceptional journey, I do think the heat and malleability of our relationships are common to most, if not all, families.

Throughout these past five years my mother and I have oscillated between adversary and ally. Whilst the kids believe we are a completely joined force they do not know of the spiky conversations where one decried and the other defended, and then vice-versa, over their latest escapades.

I remember so clearly what it was like to 16 or 17 but now I feel I am straddling tectonic plates of memory and emotion. Now, only now, do I have an inkling of the challenges of the parent in tempering the behaviour of the teen. Now! Now I know why my mother got SO cross with my sister, brother but I still understand the impotent rage of the teen denied.

But the teenage years are at an end now, for a little while at least. Time has dulled the jagged edges that my husband's breakdown and brother's accident tore into the fabric of my family.

My mother and I are less adversarial than we were. A mutual respect has grown between us, mother to mother, which I value greatly. Even so, I will do things differently with my daughter, as each generation is bound to do. As I remember the hurts of my growing up I vow that my daughter will not feel the same. I might succeed in this but I know now that she will have hurts of her own from which I can't protect her.

I do know that I will use the lessons my brother's kids and my mother have taught me and strive to be the best parent I can be for my small daughter. I would like to hope she will benefit from my having a crack at parenting teens before I was ever supposed to!

For my nephew and niece, adults they may be but parenting they still need. We have all felt the strain of the change in our circumstances. Hand on heart I have tried my best but it has not always been good enough. Getting one to uni and keeping the other out of jail are my top two achievements – perhaps they might have another view!

I wondered how to bring this story to a close when I began writing it. How to finish was puzzling me for a while.

There is no end when you're a parent though, not when they're 18 or 21 or married and having babies of their own.

From birth your influences, their memories, your lessons, their outcomes are intertwined.

Even when you're dead and gone……………

Chapter Nineteen – Adele

Having had a strong maternal instinct ever since I can remember, becoming a mother at the age of 27 was just the best thing that could have happened to me. I was so ready to settle down and be a devoted mother.

I had made a big mistake on my choice of father but I swore to myself I would be the best single mother ever and my daughter would have a nice life. I would give her all the things I didn't have for one reason or another, love would be abundant ....yes, life would be good....simple as that!

I didn't live near my family so my pregnancy was quite a lonely time. I engrossed myself in reading just about every book and magazine related to the subject and prepared the nest for my little girl.

The big day arrived. After a long and not so pleasant labour, Molly was born. My mother and a close family friend were waiting outside the delivery suite. I was alone, apart from the obvious necessary staff. I was so overcome with emotions when she was put into my arms. It was an indescribable experience. This beautiful little baby was all mine and I was now responsible for her every need. I liked the feeling. I was so ready for this new chapter. Life was wonderful.

When Molly was six months old we moved to a house near my parents. This meant she could now have the true family feeling around grandparents, aunts, uncles and cousins.

At this point I felt I would probably never have a proper relationship again and I wanted Molly to have the experience of sharing and caring for others. I decided I would like to become a voluntary foster carer. I had so much love to offer. I began the process and I was approved by the time Molly was 18 months old. Within days Jake, a two-day-old little boy, arrived. It was so exciting getting all prepared for him.

He was a lovely little baby. Molly adored him. I was involved closely with his young mother. She had hidden her pregnancy and was placing him for adoption as she had met someone new who could not accept her son. It was heart-breaking seeing this young girl in this position. The day before the adoption papers were due to be signed I brought Jake to see her for one last time and I told her to come to my home that evening with her fiancé so he could meet her son. I wanted her to be honest about her emotions as she was blatantly putting on a strong front. They came that evening and it was an evening I will never forget. Her fiancé saw the mother's face and could see the pain she was feeling inside. He lifted the baby and held him to his chest and cried. I treasure the photos of that evening. They left after an hour and late that night the mother called me. She thanked me for helping her open up and be her real self, expressing rather than suppressing her true feelings. They were going to keep the baby. I knew it was the right thing for Jake.

After some assessments by Social Services it was decided that Jake would return to his mother. That day was a very sad day for me, but also very joyous. We remained in touch. The mother married her fiancé. He adopted Jake and has been a fantastic father to him and his sister.

Molly gained a lot from this experience; we both did. My feelings as a mother were like cells multiplying within me and at times I felt I could burst with love and caring. I treasured her even more ... if that was possible. Soon there was to be a new arrival.....another hidden pregnancy, another story!

Two weeks later Ethan arrived. Another little bundle of joy graced our home whilst Social Services did an investigation into the circumstances surrounding this hidden pregnancy.

An obviously vulnerable woman in her late twenties who wanted her baby, but because Social Services were overly suspicious of who the father was she had to wait five long months before being reunited with him. She and I became friends. She confided in me and soon justice was done. She came to stay with me and learned all the basics of looking after her baby. It was a great day when she took him home. She was the best mother I had ever seen and we are still in touch. Ethan, now in his twenties, was seriously ill last year and the devotion of his mother is what saved him. I feel very privileged to be part of their story. I learnt a lot about empathy and compassion from this very humble family.

Then Gloria arrived and was to leave her mark on us forever.

Born with alcohol foetal syndrome, this tiny little girl was in such distress in her early days. The thing about having a newborn you didn't give birth to is your hormones and body clock are not prepared for the sleepless nights, and there were many of them. Because of the circumstances surrounding why Gloria was with us and the knowledge she would not be going home I bonded with her in a different way. I loved her to pieces. Molly loved her too. She was going to be staying for a while. Then Adam arrived. A little boy aged three who had been neglected. There was a lot of work to be done here but it was worth it. Within a year we were a proper little family. My family were their family. Life was busy.

This is the point at which I look back and wonder: was this a good experience or a cruel one for my own daughter?

Gloria left us when she was three and a half. She went to be adopted with one of her twelve siblings. Everyone felt this would be best for her, and after a very stressful sad time the move took place. Molly was broken hearted. We watched Gloria walk up the path to the waiting car, thinking she was going on a little trip, saying "Come on, Mummy, come on!" I was devastated. I knew I would never foster again. Soon after that Adam went to a long term foster placement, also with a sibling. Life was back to being just Molly and me. When I realised her pain I felt so guilty. I should have considered this. I didn't.

Life changed from then on and we moved to London. Another big upset for Molly but a move which I thought would be good for us. I didn't realise how hard this was for Molly, settling into a new school and leaving my parents – her grandparents – and our extended family behind. I was in a relationship and got married when Molly was nine. Everything felt right and she now had a father figure in her life. He was good to her and they bonded well. Prior to this my father was the only man in her life. She adored him. The feelings were mutual.

I then had twins, a boy and a girl. Molly was great with them. Looking back, she was pushed aside. Unintentionally, I was so busy that I overlooked signs of her unhappiness. My father died when the twins were fourteen months old. This was a really difficult time for Molly and a major turning point, sending her on an emotional rollercoaster. When the twins were two I had a baby girl. Life was so busy and Molly did a lot to help me. My marriage was breaking down and Molly's relationship with my husband was too.

There were many factors contributing to this total breakdown.

Molly and I were both extremely unhappy. I did my best to cope with having three children under 3 and Molly, who was now 12. We struggled financially and I had post-natal depression, be it for a short time, but it had an impact on us all.

By the age of 15 Molly had begun to experiment with drugs and I, believing she needed space and time with her friends, probably gave her too much freedom. I thought I was doing something good for her. I was so wrong. I never realised how she truly felt inside and drugs perhaps made her forget and feel good, at least temporarily.

Throughout all this she managed to do well in school and gain excellent GCSE results. She went to college and was soon in an abusive relationship. (I wasn't aware of this until much later.) She became pregnant and dropped out of college. I did my best to help, and stood by her. She had moved into her own place and I knew I had to step back and let her make her own choices. It's so easy to dictate when you see your child making bad decisions. I felt so helpless and frustrated. These were sad days.

Her daughter was born when she was 19 and another journey was to begin. What should have been a lovely time was marred by her drug addiction, and our whole family suffered immeasurably. No one could freely enjoy the simple day to day life. It was overshadowed by worry and anxiety and the need to protect Sandra.

It's very difficult to trust an addict, even when that addict is your beautiful kind loving caring daughter. I just wanted to be Nana, doing things that grandparents do. Instead I was on standby 24/7, constantly worrying, sleepless nights and an overwhelming anxiety. I loved my daughter so much but had a duty to this little baby, my granddaughter.

I did everything I possibly could to get help for Molly, but she always slipped back. Her health was affected. I did a lot of research into the drug she was using, going as far as talking to parents in America whose children were using or had used the same drug. I was frightened. I explained to Molly what I believed was going to happen if she didn't stop. I never got through to her, at least not then. By the time she realised I was right, it was too late.

She was very ill for approximately three years but continued to use.

She had major surgery when Sandra was five. This was the worst day of my life – and hers too. Her life has changed dramatically. Thankfully she is no longer using and realises the damage she has done to herself. She has so many regrets. I feel the pain every day and keep it to myself.

I look back over the last 25 years of mothering and sometimes wish I could have that time over again. I think of all the things I would do differently and on a daily basis I absorb what I can only describe as a pain of failing to protect my children from the big bad world we live in. With my abundance of love and wanting to spoil my children, I believe I have done them a great disservice.

Irrespective of the many mistakes I have made by loving my children so much, the one consolation is that they all know how much I love them. I make sure I tell them even at times when it's difficult to say. The foster children have a greater appreciation and respect for me than my own children. I gave them what they needed at a time in their lives when they couldn't get it from their own mothers. They see this as a great privilege and feel my love for them as a bonus. As for my own natural children, they look upon my love and my efforts to give them as much as I possibly can as my duty. They have disrespect for me at times; they blame me for spoiling them.

I feel a big change happening now as they are all at different stages of teenage development. My persistence in loving them unconditionally, even though it is overshadowed with a deep hurt inside me, is beginning to play a part in their changing behaviour, which is notably improving. Perhaps they are now ready to take responsibility for their futures. My love still flows and I still feel the need to envelop them in this. It is time for a progressive phase in our lives as a family. I am hopeful we will strengthen and blossom as we rise from the ashes.

Chapter Twenty – Susan

I have been a foster carer with my husband since the summer of 2009. Our own children were getting ready to fly the nest, we had the room and felt that we had something to offer. Waiting for our first placement to arrive, I felt a mixture of excitement, anticipation and a little anxiety. How would they find us? Would they like us? Was everything ready, so it was welcoming but not overwhelming?

After nearly six months of the application process and training we were ready. Well, as ready as we ever would be! We had been told that the first few weeks or even months with the child was known as the honeymoon period as it is often not until the child is sure enough of you that they feel comfortable enough to express their emotions. Often, these children are full of confusion and anger and you are the target.

I think the honeymoon period with our first placement, a boy who was eight years old, lasted just a few days! As is often the way we got very sketchy information, but I remember he had been described as liking crafts and gardening. "Great," I thought, imagining us creating stuff at the kitchen table or planting flowers in the garden. Talk about rosy coloured spectacles! We later discovered he had been excluded from school and his behaviour was very challenging, as I was about to find out. It was a beautiful summer's evening and I was at a friend's house when I got a frantic phone call from my husband to come home quickly. I arrived home to discover my husband with a bleeding lip in a standoff situation. The child was grabbing and smashing anything he could get his hands on. I sidled around the room and gathered some precious items into an empty laundry basket for safety, along with the kitchen knives. This rage lasted about four hours before he finally burnt himself out. Cause unknown. This became a daily occurrence. We didn't really have a chance to parent this child. He certainly did not allow me to mother him in a conventional way, and we felt much more like prison officers, just trying our best to keep some sort of order and keep him and us safe. We called him our 'baptism of fire' and if I am honest I was more than relieved to see him go to his new placement at the end of the summer holidays.

Our next placement was two sisters who came to us straight from their troubled home. They had been told by their family to screw us for everything they could get. Not the best start!

After being with us for a year or so one of our foster children asked if she could call me Mum. The social worker explained that as long as she was clear that I wasn't her real birth mum, but her foster mum, it would be alright. I was ok with it at first and I know it was necessary to help her to feel the same as most of her friends and for a sense of belonging. However, as we hit a rocky patch along with puberty, I found I didn't feel comfortable with her calling me Mum as it was so loaded. By this, I mean I live up to my own definition of 'mum' in every sense of the word to my own birth children. I would do anything for them and go to the ends of the earth for them. However, I didn't have this deep bond, affection and love for this child and I felt guilty that I wasn't living up to my own definition of being a mum. It would have been easier for me if she called me by my Christian name but I can't change that now. I am learning to not feel guilty but to see that I am her role model as a mother figure and it is just a name.

This and other little things are what makes it so complicated being a family that fosters. The children are part of your family but at the same time they are not. You have to be professional in your own home and yet it is your home. You have to have your house checked for safety, provide annual boiler certificates, have two or more unannounced visits by social workers, a written fire policy and loads more quite intrusive visits and checks. Your life is thrown open to a whole host of people and it can be very invasive. Sometimes it doesn't feel like a home, your own sanctuary from the world, as the world is free to visit and inspect at will. You have to quantify that you are providing activities outside of school; you are checked that you are taking them to the dentist every six months. Sometimes it does feel like you are not just sharing your life with someone else's children but Social Services too!

As a mother, the unknown nature of the outcome of each placement can make it difficult to give it your all and I find that it is necessary to hold something of myself back as a way of protecting myself. Even if you are approved as a child's long term foster carer until they are grown up, it doesn't mean that this will be the case. The child could decide that they are unhappy living with you and your rules and asked to be moved. They may make a false allegation (more common than you would think) or they may be moved by the local authority for any number of reasons. This can be tough on you as a carer trying to get the balance right between nurturing the children and protecting yourself emotionally.

When I started fostering with my husband, I knew it would be no walk in the park and our birth children (then 18 and 20) were very supportive. In reality, understandably, they found it much harder. Both were still at living at home and I found it difficult to manage the dynamics between them all. Maybe it was not my job to try and make sure they all got on, but if I am honest I had hoped that we would become one big happy family. Our foster children didn't always make it easy for my birth children and they would often display attention seeking behaviour, start arguments, or sidle up to me and give me a hug as if to say "she is my mum now".

It is a really strange and difficult job being a foster carer, especially for us women who probably wouldn't have become carers unless we had strong mothering / nurturing instincts. Often these children can be pretty damaged emotionally and may have missed out on the vital nurturing that they require to become secure and happy individuals. As a carer this can be frustrating as you see those making poor choices and rejecting opportunities that you know could make life much better and easier for them. While disruptive behaviours in your own children are stressful, you have that bond with them which formed before they were born. But with foster children you haven't had that opportunity and often you are trying to build a relationship when you are only getting grief.

Despite all the challenges there is a truly wonderful side to being a foster mother, such as the first time I saw one of the children laugh with pure joy as I pushed her higher and higher on a swing. To see that she was able to be a child: relaxed, happy and safe … you realise in those moments that you are doing something really worthwhile and amazing!

We have been privileged to experience many 'firsts' with our foster children and built up lots of happy memories together. I was so excited to take them to the seaside for the first time and to see their faces light up when they had their first paddle in the sea; I shared in the triumphant look on the youngest one's face when she finally plucked up the courage to splash in a puddle in her new Wellington boots.

Some of the happiest memories are of the simple things, such as seeing their pride when they seek out your face at the school play and they know you are there, just for them, because you care. Or hearing them sing in the bath, or seeing them skip home from school hand in hand with their best friend.

To be a foster mum I think you need to have a big heart, a strong support network and know that while love will not solve everything, it will certainly help.

Chapter Twenty-One – Rosie

When my first son was born in 1981, new mothers usually stayed in hospital for about a week. In the bed next to me was another new mother. We chatted and she told me she was a social worker. I told her I'd been brought up in care.

I already knew about social workers; I'd had a few in my time, and even a couple of good ones. Perhaps I was being unfair: their role is really difficult – dealing with children who they have removed from their families. Children who, as well as being needy for love and acceptance, also look to social workers for some sort of permanence and please God, not more rejection. Yet that will usually come with the end of the relationship with the social worker. At the time I was in hospital I thought about the social worker and wondered what it was about people like her that made me feel so shit about myself. However, I digress; after learning that I'd been brought up in care this particular one was amazed by my mothering skills. "Like a duck to water," she said. "You've taken to motherhood like a duck to water." She was struggling: her breasts were tiny and the baby wouldn't feed. She cried buckets all over that tiny thing, calling for nurses to assist her, ecstatic if the baby latched on for a second and inconsolable as it fell off again, it too crying, frustrated and hungry. Eventually it just cried all the time.

I liked this duck to water image. I imagined it, this duck sliding onto the water, always buoyant, never sinking. I felt worthy as a human being for the first time in my life. This social worker – this woman, and others like her, who were normally in such control and had so much power over me and others like me – was out of control, and I felt for her. But I also felt chuffed, proud and all puffed up like a bright and beautiful turquoise-blue peacock. I was a mother and full of the most amazing maternal feelings of love for my child. Overwhelmed. Not that it was overwhelming for me, just that I was overwhelmed with the urge to give and receive love. I changed my son's nappy with ease, I washed and bathed him while the social worker called for the nurse, worried about her son's head dropping, worried she would drown him. I was a lioness, and when the nurse gave my son the heel-prick test and made him scream, that tiny defenceless beautiful baby, I wanted to scream too. Of course I didn't. I held him, my son, snuggled him into my breast, loved him with all my being.

I was a success, I was a mother and I was married. Society couldn't look down its nose at my child like it had at me.

If my mother had loved me the way I loved my son, I felt the most devastating sorrow for her. For what she had gone through. What must that have been like, to give up your child? Having to give me up because it was 1958 and unmarried mothers were the scum of British society back then. Her parents had already told her, "Don't bring that bastard baby back here." The thought filled me with panic, anxiety. I kept waking all through the night, checking and re-checking that my baby was still there. I thought I understood, maybe for the first time, why my mother had killed herself. If I had to give up my child I would die. Her pain, her suffering, all those pills to control it, to control her, and her final act of rebellion. I even imagined her talking to those pills: "Well, if this is what you want, here goes. I'll take all of them and fuck the lot of you." I wondered if her wound, her pain, was like mine?

Those of us with the wound don't walk through life; we float, our anchor, our heritage gone. Occasionally we may stop for a while, trying a new mooring, but often, with that gnashing, humungous sore we don't stay, and so we fly away, up and over the rooftops, where the pain subsides and we can find some sort of peace – though of course it doesn't last.

The problem for me was that when she died, she took all my heritage with her. All that knowledge about me, my father, into the grave. And the problem with knowledge is too little can lead to all sorts of fiction. Too much of it can change history, our history, our fictional lives; the lives we create between the pages of other's stories – or the glamorous, Technicolor dream that we see on the big screen of life. Back then when my first son was born, I didn't have that knowledge. I hadn't read my files. I didn't know that my mother barely visited the residential nursery where I'd been placed, and when I contracted a life-threatening disease and nearly died in hospital a few months later, she was busy re-creating a new life with an expectant new baby and a handsome father. I didn't know this then. At that time I still felt sorry for my unwell mother. How can you be angry with a mentally unstable woman? Now I stop to think about it, I don't think her wound, her pain, was like mine.

I stayed in the residential nursery waiting for a mother and a father. I couldn't be put up for adoption because my mother was mad – another taboo in those days. So adverts were put in The Universe, The Catholic Times and The Catholic Herald, just below the 'grateful thanks to Our Lady of Perpetual Succour, the Holy Family and all the Saints for favours received' and just above 'Human Hair wanted 12ins or over; cash by return'. The date at the top of the page? April Fool's day, 1960! But nobody wanted a mad child who couldn't be adopted.

Then one day a recently bereaved widow came to visit. After a few more visits, she took me home. I would be with her for two years. My first memories of life are of Joan, not of the residential nursery. I was two and a half by the time I went to stay with her. So she was all I knew. I called her Aunty Joan but I wanted to call her Mummy, like the other children did. She had two grown up sons and I was the apple of everybody's eye – except when I had tantrums or ate soap.

We had holidays, I started nursery school, and Aunty Joan spoilt me and made me sugar sandwiches for my mid-morning snack. She grew to love me and I grew to love her. I was bridesmaid to her eldest son and had a little girl crush on the younger one. Joan took me to the park nearly every day and she spoke about robins and how they were the souls of dead people come to visit. The day I went to visit my mother, there were dark clouds and rain in the air and I thought that was why we hadn't gone to the park.

The second time the social worker came to take me for a visit to my mother, I screamed and screamed until Aunty Joan agreed she would accompany us. When we arrived she waited a little while until my attention was taken by my new brother and she crept out of the house. She did the same thing on the day I was taken there to live permanently with my new mother, stepfather and younger brother.

I was told this enormous, lethargic woman was my mother. I didn't feel any connection with her at all, and it seemed to me that she felt the same way. Even at four and a half I could see that my younger brother was the apple of her eye. At five and a half she would go out for the day and leave me to look after my brother and a new-born. Even then I can remember the feelings of love I had for that tiny baby. At six and a half, she took all three of us to the local clinic where she told them she was going shopping. She never came back. We were taken to the local police station where a policewoman caught me sucking on my brother's bottle. I lied, said I hadn't, and she gave me a lecture on the perils of lying.

My first brother was taken by my grandparents to stay with them. My stepfather took the baby and me home with him. I don't know how he coped as he was drunk most of the time. We were eventually put back into foster care although unfortunately not with Aunty Joan. After a few weeks my stepfather collected us. This was with a ready-made foster family, where I soon found my place. The natural children were of course the favourites; I was Cinderella.

After two years with an abusive stepfather and a mentally unstable mother, I was pretty fucked up and the mental and physical cruelty of the foster parents was the icing on the cake.

Apparently my mother had bumped into an old boyfriend whom she still loved – whatever love was to her. I don't know what happened between them but after some time, possibly a year, I was placed back with her in a bedsit – just the two of us. She was heading for another breakdown and I received the brunt of that instability.

Thank goodness after that, I was taken into care again. I was placed in a massive children's home with about fifty kids. I stayed there for a year and was eventually moved to a small children's home where I stayed for eight years until I was sixteen.

From birth until two and a half I had had no parenting. I'd had a loving foster mother for just two years until I was four and a half, abusive parenting for another three years and then residential care until I was sixteen. Despite my lack of mothering as a child, I was able to give my children proper care and unconditional love.

And the strange thing was, I took to it like a duck to water.[11]

---

[11] Rosie Canning is co-founder of Greenacre Writers. She completed an MA Writing at Middlesex and is working on an autobiographical novel about a care leaver.

PART THREE

The Journey to Self

Chapter Twenty-Two

There comes a point when we have to heal from our traumas, whether we become aware that we are in so much pain that we can't take it any more as we watch every area of our life be defined by our experiences, or because we are forced to change through a life-changing event.

I believe there are people who manage to get through life without dealing with what has happened to them. The warning signs that things have to be dealt with and have to change usually present so loudly and clearly that I am amazed when people are able to ignore them.

Needing to heal, to change, to deal with what has happened tends to present in very visible ways, such as:

- The need to self-medicate (alcohol, drugs, food, sex) and the effects of all of those things being 'used' and over-used
- A negative relationship pattern
- Poor health

The less visible tend to be:

- Feelings of isolation and aloneness

- Depression
- A sense of disconnect

This is not an exhaustive list, of course, but there is a high personal price for staying in the pain and it has never been one I was prepared to pay. Driven to take the journey to self, the journey back to me, I continuously strive to be the very best version of myself.

Essentially, the pain of change, of getting 'well', has to be less painful than the pain of staying the same.

This is very challenging at times – and incredibly rewarding. Writing this book has taken me to depths that I thought even just a year before that I would not be able to bear emotionally. It has taken to me to what has felt like the very edge of myself, yet I know that the more I continue on this journey, the more peace I have within myself, the more joyful and rewarding my life becomes and the more people I can help and support. Whether that is in some small way or in a much greater way, it matters not.

The really good news is that we can heal from whatever it is that has happened to us. We can find who we are truly are without being the mess that our hurts may have made us. We can learn how to have strong friendships, positive relationships with our loved ones; we can be conscious and loving parents, and contribute in a positive way to our communities.

The stories in this book demonstrate that but I would add that I subscribe to the belief that we are made up of all the things that have happened to us. The journey to self is not about getting rid of these things or denying them or making them vanish. They are with us always, like little imprints on our soul.

When a child has been abused, for example, that imprint is with them forever. Ask anyone who has recently been patronised by the media and had their experience of being abused called 'historic abuse'; there is nothing historic about it for the adult living with it.

To understand this better, think of all the wonderful memories and experiences we carry with us, whether we remember them consciously or they have left imprints on our soul that tell us we are special and wanted and valued.

In the same way as all the positive loving things that have happened to us cannot be removed, nor can the hurt or the damage; it is a part of us. It is a part of the beautiful fabric of what makes us unique.

It is for this reason that I am passionate about the role we have as individuals, as professionals and as a society in valuing and supporting positive pregnancy and childbirth, helping parents to *consciously* parent and the potential to be found in positive early years development.

That exploration is probably for another book but it would be remiss of me not to mention that the greatest gift we can give ourselves is being part of the solution and seeing healing in the wider context. Breaking the cycle was one of my most powerful driving factors in my own experience of mothering.

We can grow and learn to live peacefully with our 'imprints' as opposed to living with them in a way that defines who we are and causes us more hurt as we repeat patterns of destruction that validate the negative things we have learned through trauma rather than drawing on anything positive that has happened.

Whether you are supporting someone on this 'recovery' or you are very much in the throes of it yourself, there are some helpful personal qualities required to assist when embarking upon this and you'll discover that you have them within you even if you didn't know it!

There is much spoken – usually in sound bites in poorly written self help books or posters on your Facebook wall – about the past. Don't go there, we don't live there, look forward, never look back. The past is seen as something to be avoided; by working through your past, you haven't moved on.

I find this quite unhelpful because the truth is you can't move on if you keep avoiding it, not really. It will always have a hold on you in some way. Looking back is also a great aid in measuring where we've come from. On that basis alone, the past is not to be ignored. The key is to ensure that it doesn't define you.

However, there are certain things that we need in great big dollops, not only to help us embark upon recovering but also to be able to stay in a place of growth and recovery every day.

- **Courage**

The definition of courage is enlightening.

"Courage – The state or quality of mind or spirit that enables one to face danger, fear, or vicissitudes with self-possession, confidence, and resolution; bravery. Courage is the ability and willingness to confront fear, pain, danger, uncertainty, or intimidation."

How many of us think we are not courageous? When you see this as the definition, how many of you now know that you are truly courageous?

Facing up to where we have been and where we are now and using that to shape a better future for ourselves requires courage, especially when we think of it as a 'willingness to confront fear'. If we're going into the unknown that can create a feeling of anxiety and fear, not least because we are unable to know what is on the other side of that journey.

- **Resilience**

This is my favourite one, as we can all have this: it is a skill, so it can be learned. If you have been through the mill a bit, then you'll have lots of it, because you'll have needed it to get to this very moment in your life where you are reading this book.

The definition of resilience is:

"The ability to recover quickly from illness, change, or misfortune; buoyancy. The property of a material that enables it to resume its original shape or position after being bent, stretched, or compressed; elasticity."

Resilience is what allows us to deal with what life throws at us without denying that it is happening.

- **Honesty**

Honesty is defined as *"The quality or condition of being honest; integrity. Truthfulness; sincerity: in all honesty."*

Without being honest with ourselves, it is very hard to confront and deal with anything. This can be hard to do, especially when we can get confused with what we think we know, what we think happened, what we remember and what we don't remember but can feel.

Learning to be honest with ourselves is about developing a loving and forgiving inner relationship with ourselves that can be translated into our relationships when we feel safe enough to be vulnerable.

- **Love**

"A deep, tender, ineffable feeling of affection and solicitude toward a person, such as that arising from kinship, recognition of attractive qualities, or a sense of underlying oneness."

The goal is to have this deep and tender feeling of affection for ourselves: learning to love ourselves, all of ourselves is the cornerstone to recovery. It can be very hard. But I believe it's essential for us to move on. Where we haven't had this shown to us, taught to us, we have to learn how to do it and give it to ourselves.

- **Vulnerability**

This is the ability to show another person who you are without fear. I searched for a definition that I liked but I couldn't find one. Brene Brown[12] has written on the power of vulnerability and listening to her talks will tell you just about everything you need to know about being vulnerable and the benefits of doing so. For me, I see vulnerability as

---

[12] Brenebrown.com

the point where courage, resilience, honesty and love all meet. [13]

The next part of the jigsaw is understanding where the self and the damaged self starts and ends.

---

[13] In my first book Soul Journey, I cover in much more detail these elements of recovery and how to apply them in your life.

Chapter Twenty-Three – Unravelling The Unconscious

Over the years I have experienced different therapies, read many books, trained in my own field, been on a 12-step programme and lived a life dedicated to being in a place of 'recovery'; I've lived life from the view of being the very best version of myself. But still there were places I could not reach to heal. In earlier chapters I have spoken of the wound and in having imprints of damage on my soul. Talking about this particular aspect of myself, in a therapeutic sense, has not been helpful to me. I have an internal need to understand things and then to articulate them and I could not access this internal space with words at all. I found this immensely frustrating.

I did not know how to heal myself when I couldn't get to the very place that I knew was there and was hurting. Every time I almost touched it with my fingertips, it slipped away.

As I progressed in my own journey, I came to realise that there were two places of hurt that were still affecting my life that I couldn't get to through all the work I had done during the previous couple of decades.

Firstly, there were the hurts and pains that I needed to deal with that I couldn't access. I came to understand that the initial wound happened before I had words and therefore I was unable to articulate how I was feeling – the damage done by non-attachment for six weeks was clinging tightly to the framework of my soul.

Secondly, I needed to get to the things that I had internalised prior to having the capacity for reason beyond messy childhood interpretation. This had created messages within me that ran so deeply that not only could I not get to them, I was barely aware they were there. In all my awareness, in all my work, the story of me was tucked away neatly in a set of beliefs that I would adamantly deny existed for no other reason than I didn't believe they were there! For me I believe this occurred through the messages that I would have collected as a 13 year old being thrown out of home: I am not worthy, I do not deserve love; it was all my fault; I must have been really bad.

Much of the latter has been dealt with in many ways in recovery, but the action taken in order to do that to me was from another person and is an action that I cannot comprehend, however I look at it, through whatever lens and from whatever angle.

So there are two areas within my unconscious that told me a story: a story that I am not wanted, not lovable, not worthy. It is this story that I absolutely needed to work with or I was never going to be able to have a loving healthy relationship with another. I knew this in my heart, so the search was vital to me.

*

So how can we get to this un-conscious and sub-conscious pain? I found out rather by accident. Having been involved in holistic health[14] professionally since 2006 and as a way of life on and off for years, I was familiar with many different forms of complementary and alternative health therapies and I mix with many people who live in that way.

In September 2010, I was at an event held by a friend where taster sessions in different therapies were available. I had my eye on a woman giving Kinesiology,[15] something I had not previously tried. The sessions were for just fifteen minutes and I was fortunate enough to get the very last slot with her. During the session, my self-worth came up, and so I needed to say a series of statements. One of them was "I deserve food and love." This had been identified as something I needed help with. Two hours later, having been taken to my knees sobbing because I couldn't actually

---

[14] By holistic health, I mean adopting an approach to health and well-being that addresses the body, mind and spirit or the physical, emotional/mental and spiritual aspects of self. By spirit or spiritual, I am not making a reference to anything religious. I'm talking about the essence of who you are; the core self.

[15] Kinesiology uses gentle muscle-monitoring techniques to access the subconscious mind and gain information about your current issues and what is needed to help your body, mind and spirit to restore balance.

say the sentence in the context of this session, I learnt in that moment that some things are just buried so deeply, our conscious selves can deny their very existence.

If you had asked me whether I felt deserving of food and love I would have said of course! But deep down, I had not resolved this issue of worth. It was this knowledge that helped me to understand that to get to the hurt and pain I couldn't articulate, I needed to go within on a completely different level – and my journey took a new turn.

I discovered Reiki[16] and over the course of the next two years became a Reiki Master. I made this a way of life for me.

Personally I have found great healing from using therapies that I don't necessarily understand, that I can't intellectualise and that don't require me to know what needs to be healed. I believe there are many routes and roads to becoming well and healing from pain; in fact there are as many routes as there are people. I always advise people to try different things, be open-minded and see what feels right for you. There is no prescription in this sense; it is essentially about taking responsibility for your

---

[16] Reiki is a technique or therapy that aims to reduce stress, promote relaxation and encourage a person to heal. The theory behind Reiki is that it is possible to heal a person or increase their life force energy by using the techniques learned or acquired by a Reiki practitioner. The way in which Reiki is administered is a form of 'laying on hands'. However, Reiki is an entirely non-intrusive therapy.

pain and making a decision to go and do something about it before it defines you and prevents you from living the life you could be living.

I'm not sure that I could have got to the core of myself, which was wrapped in my unconscious, without having done all of the work that lay ahead before I arrived there. I would suggest not. There have been a lot of layers to plough through! Your journey may be different. Taking the first step to our best selves is the best gift we can give, not only to us but to the people who love us. It is not what we went through that defines us but rather how we got through it. That is what defines us as a person.

Chapter Twenty-Four – Conclusion

The phrase 'duck to water' makes a couple of appearances in this book. The idea that much of what we do as a mother is instinctive, yet we either 'take to it' like the floating duck or we don't, presents an interesting thought to me. So is it instinctive or do we have an element of choice whether we take to it in all its glory?

As I explained earlier, I certainly found most of it to be instinctive but I didn't take to it like a 'duck to water'. I had no idea what I needed, who to ask for that which I didn't understand or how I should feel. As I looked around the various rooms of 'mother' – ante-natal groups, post-natal coffees, doctors' waiting rooms, other mums – they all had the rule book, it seemed. Here I was again without the bloody 'how to' book of life with the section on parenting in it! How did that happen?

Breastfeeding, protection of my baby and love in its purest form; yes. That was mine, no rule book required. My instinct.

So if we accept that we all sit on different places on the 'instinct' spectrum and we all have different levels of support and knowledge, coupled with personal life experiences that range from utterly beautiful to downright traumatic, we start to engage with mothering as the complex life experience that it is. We then start to have a more empathic response to the difficulties that many mothers face when presented with a pregnancy, a birth, a baby (and then of course all that follows – and for some women that might involve not being with their baby at all).

The stories explored here offer us much in the way of learning and understanding this complex experience which is so often presented to us by society as a one-dimensional cartoon.

The foster mother or the adopting mother must often feel ignored as their absence in the cartoon stares back in all its glory. Is the 'duck to water' option available to them too? Is the act of mothering itself, the doing of it, open to us when we haven't birthed a child?

I found a beautiful write-up somewhere a couple of years ago while surfing around on the internet about mothering which includes looking at mothering in the wider sense than birthing and I rather liked it because of that. It opens up the idea of mothering to its origins: Mother Earth, and how we can all practise this beautiful gift of extended mothering. Beautiful ways of viewing the word mother can bring many people some peace. These altered perspectives enable us to understand mother and mothering as a different way of viewing the world.

Communities can mother if we open up this understanding. I found this definition and origin of mothering that I kept as I knew I might need it sometime and this seems the most likely place for it to go.

"The lovely month of May has a Goddess all its own – in fact its namesake. Maia, eldest of the seven Pleiades, is sometimes folded in with the Goddess Gaia, even though in Greek mythology the two were separate. The name Maia has several possible meanings, including "midwife," "good mother," "foster mother," or "aunty." It also means "great" or "more" in Latin. Variations on her name include Maiesta, Maja, Majestas, and Majesty. She is often associated as a Goddess of Spring and renewal, and therefore with the Goddesses Gaia, Maia Maiestas (Roman), Fauna, Flora, Bona Dea, and Opis (or Ops).

Maia, in addition to being the eldest sister, was the mother to two important deities in ancient Greece: Hermes and Iris.

Historically, Maia was honoured by the Romans with the sacrifice of a sow on Her worship day, May 1st, which was conducted by a "flamen" or priest of Vulcan. She was also honoured on May 15 with her son, which the dedication day of Mercury's temple on the Aventine. In her role as Vulcan's wife, she was also honoured at Volcanalia, on August 23, a festival to ward off the fires caused by the heat of the long, hot summer. Interestingly, men were excluded from her worship precincts – perhaps because of her associations with birth, fecundity, and midwifery.

Any celebration of Beltane is, by its very nature, appropriate to Maia, since it's a celebration of the fertility of the Earth and the energies of growth, birth, regeneration, and springtime. Maia could be helpful in magic to enhance creativity or fertility, or in setting a course of action with an energetically congruent goal as an outcome. She also represents the transition from Maiden to Mother Goddess as well as fire, which means that "all acts of love and pleasure" are Her rituals."[17]

May then, is the month of The Mother, in whatever form that may be.

My aim was to provide a wider lens with which to see through and to explore the outcomes for us as the child and as the mother when shown the different circumstances life presents us with that do not include the very narrow lens offered to mothers in the media.

*

Writing this book has been enlightening and harrowing all at once. It is only at this point in my life that I am willing to accept that I am defined by that first relationship, the relationship with mother. My anger would never have allowed me to do this prior to the explorations that I have undertaken in order to actually write about this subject; written from my wound, the initial scar, that which I have

---

[17] Source unknown.

never been able to articulate as it lay so deeply hidden, yet always present.

My sometimes strange relationships, decisions I have taken, places I have been and beliefs I have had stem from this beginning in life, even when I had no idea that this was case.

Whether I have been in communication with my mother, whether that has been a lot or a little, whether we have not been speaking (and we have had many periods of silence), whether I have felt forgiveness or felt peace, whether I have been enraged or in despair, my thoughts have always, to varying degrees, been aware of it all. It never leaves me, not for any length of time anyway.

I cannot escape this place in my internal self that wants to be mothered and after that, fathered and sistered and brothered. But I only have a mother; a mother I cannot accept as my own mother, although I have tried so hard over the years. I am trapped by the conscious and sub conscious knowledge that I was abandoned by her not once but twice. Even though I sympathise with her trauma as an unmarried woman in 1969, pregnant at 21 and in Nazareth House doing the light housework expected, I have no sympathy for her at all with the vision I have of the 13 year old with two bin bags of belongings and all that followed. However hard things were, I cannot accept the woman who changed the course of my life so dramatically, enabling experiences to happen to me that I would never wish upon anyone – and that I shall take with me to my grave.

The forgiveness and acceptance that I work on daily are in a bid to find some peace for myself on this matter, for that is what forgiveness is: an opportunity to set ourselves free and find peace. Forgiveness is for me.

So much of what I have written with regards to how I feel about it all has been written about endless times. This may give you some insight into the constant, almost silent background noise that this relationship is for me. My battle with it would be pitiful for a bystander to watch but I am happy that I can be honest about it now rather than carrying the added burden of shame along with the trauma itself.

*

This cycle is present from the beginning to the end of time. It is the very creation of life and as such the unravelling of it is a constant for many of us, whether as the child and/or as the mother.

In the process of exploration there are some fundamentals in the recovery of any trauma that I would highlight.

- Self-care and self-protection
- Learning how to communicate and express ourselves in a loving and kind way

- Understanding what it is we need and then giving that to ourselves

In short, the responsibility for healing lies within ourselves, whatever our starting point. The deep need we may have for someone else to acknowledge and take responsibility for their part in our trauma may never come. The continued search for it will only ever prevent us from becoming well, understanding our recovery and developing our resilience.

Ultimately, it may often be the case that being the gift of life is all there is to the relationship. Ultimately, there comes a point where it may be the case that that has to be enough.

*

About the Author

Keynote Speaker ~ Author ~ Mentor~ Mother of Teens ~
Professional Trainer ~ Coffee Snob

Lisa Cherry has spent over twenty years in social work, education and social inclusion settings working with families, young people and individuals in distress. In 2010, Lisa embarked upon a new direction of working with individuals with a sharp focus on awareness, transformation, personal responsibility and healing and The Awareness Revolution Ltd was born.

An international blogger, speaker, published author and trainer, Lisa helps beginner writers to remove the emotional blocks that may be preventing them from starting on writing projects, working on rebuilding confidence, finding their voice and learning how to feel safe in order to express difficult emotional trauma.

Lisa works with people in groups or individually and is the creator of Whatever!® Youth Coaching, a national programme for vulnerable young people, particularly those who are leaving care, working with them to help them transit into adulthood and giving them the tools to create better outcomes.

Through all her learning, Lisa has developed a way of working that reflects a unique skill set that has been further developed through continued training in the areas of holistic health, reiki, counselling and coaching.

She has a personal journey in sobriety and has been in recovery for over 20 years. She has written and published two other books: Soul Journey, which focuses on overcoming adversity; and The Brightness of Stars, which charts the adult voices of those who were children in the UK care system. This book has become widely read by student social workers as well as those working with children or wishing to understand children in care on a deeper level.

Lisa is regularly invited to speak at universities, writers' groups, business networking events, conferences and women's groups in the UK and Europe and has been described as "an engaging, inspiring and thought-provoking speaker."

www.lisacherry.co.uk

www.whateveryouthcoaching.co.uk

Email: lisa@lisacherry.co.uk

Twitter: @_lisacherry

Facebook: www.facebook.com/lisacherry.author